CALVINISM AND THE POLITICAL ORDER

CALVINISM
and the
POLITICAL
ORDER

Essays Prepared for the
Woodrow Wilson Lectureship of
The National Presbyterian Center
Washington, D. C.

George L. Hunt, Editor

John T. McNeill, Consulting Editor

THE WESTMINSTER PRESS

PHILADELPHIA

PUBLISHED BY THE WESTMINSTER PRESS ®

PHILADELPHIA, PENNSYLVANIA

PRINTED IN THE UNITED STATES OF AMERICA

The Woodrow Wilson Lectures
of
The National Presbyterian Church and Center

The Woodrow Wilson Lectures have been sponsored by the Council for The National Presbyterian Church and Center, an agency of the General Assembly of The United Presbyterian Church in the United States of America. It is one of the programs conceived and executed by the Council to make the principles of Presbyterianism exalted and vital in current life.

The Council expresses its appreciation to Rev. George L. Hunt, D.D., who secured the authors-lecturers and edited this book, and to Prof. John T. McNeill, who has given valuable assistance as consulting editor.

The lecture series would not have been possible without the interest of Walter N. Maguire, of Stamford, Connecticut. Mr. Maguire is a member of the Council, and through The Maguire Foundation, Inc., he has made the entire project possible.

The lectures were delivered under the auspices of The National Presbyterian Center at the following places:

"John Calvin on Civil Government" at Wayne Presbyterian Church, Wayne, Pennsylvania (November 24, 1963)

"Philip Mornay and the Huguenot Challenge to Absolutism" at the Covenant Presbyterian Church, Charlotte, North Carolina (April 29, 1964)

"Samuel Rutherford: The Law and the King" at McCormick Theological Seminary, Chicago, Illinois (April 23, 1964)

"The Puritan Ethic and the Spirit of American Democracy" at the First Presbyterian Church, Stamford, Connecticut (January 19, 1964)

"John Locke: Heir of Puritan Political Theorists" at the Fifth Avenue Presbyterian Church, New York, New York (December 8, 1963)

"John Witherspoon on Church and State" at the 175th General Assembly of The United Presbyterian Church in the U.S.A., Des Moines, Iowa (May 20, 1963)

"Abraham Lincoln and Calvinism" at the First Presbyterian Church, Springfield, Illinois (January 12, 1964)

"Woodrow Wilson: Presbyterian in Government" at The National Presbyterian Church, Washington, D.C. (November 21, 1963)

The second chapter, by Dr. McNeill, and the tenth chapter, by Dr. Hunt, were not first presented as lectures.

Lowell Russell Ditzen

Director, The National Presbyterian Center
Washington, D.C.

Contents

Contents

Contributors

Sydney E. Ahlstrom, who contributed Chapter 5, "The Puritan Ethic and the Spirit of American Democracy," is professor of church history and American history, Yale Divinity School, New Haven, Connecticut.

Paul T. Fuhrmann, who contributed Chapter 3, "Philip Mornay and the Huguenot Challenge to Absolutism," is professor of church history, Columbia Theological Seminary, Decatur, Georgia.

Winthrop S. Hudson, who contributed Chapter 6, "John Locke: Heir of Puritan Political Theorists," is professor of the history of Christianity, Colgate Rochester Divinity School, Rochester, New York.

George L. Hunt, who contributed Chapter 10, "Our Calvinist Heritage in Church and State," is senior minister of the Fanwood Presbyterian Church, Fanwood, New Jersey, and executive secretary, Consultation on Church Union.

Arthur S. Link, who contributed Chapter 9, "Woodrow Wilson: Presbyterian in Government," is professor of history and director of the Woodrow Wilson Papers, Princeton University, Princeton, New Jersey.

J. F. Maclear, who contributed Chapter 4, "Samuel Rutherford: The Law and the King," is professor of history, University of Minnesota, Duluth, Minnesota.

John T. McNeill, who contributed Chapter 1, "Calvinism and European Politics in Historical Perspective," and Chapter 2, "John Calvin on Civil Government," is professor emeritus of church history, Union Theological Seminary, New York City.

James Hastings Nichols, who contributed Chapter 7, "John Witherspoon on Church and State," is professor of modern European church history, Princeton Theological Seminary, Princeton, New Jersey.

William J. Wolf, who contributed Chapter 8, "Abraham Lincoln and Calvinism," is professor of theology, Episcopal Theological School, Cambridge, Massachusetts.

Chapter I
Calvinism and European Politics
in Historical Perspective
By John T. McNeill

The names that throng the histories of political theory are not the names of politicians or statesmen, but of philosophers, law scholars, and theologians. If we survey the literature of politics in the West from Cicero's *De republica* (56 B.C.) to Bodin's *De la république* (1576), we see that it was almost entirely the work of Christian writers with theological presuppositions. Contributors to it, in fact, included virtually all the eminent figures among the church fathers, Scholastics, and Reformers.

Since the church and the political state were everywhere in intimate contact, it was inevitable that theological writers should make political theory a province of theology. Almost without exception these writers were, however, sufficiently acquainted (directly or indirectly) with the classical philosophers to be able to utilize the political ideas of Plato, Aristotle, Cicero, Seneca, or Plutarch, skillfully blending these with the doctrines of the church. They were also men fully alive to the contemporary political conditions. In Augustine's *City of God,* John of Salisbury's *Policraticus,* and the *De regimini principum* of Aquinas—to mention three representative works —we are aware of responses to the special stresses of the fifth, the twelfth, and the thirteenth century respectively.

The Christian authors of works of this class never hesitated to reach back into the pre-Christian era for political illumination, but the classical influence upon them was

by no means a purely secularistic element. The ancient
writers may often have been uncertain about the gods, but
they were not disposed to deny the divine authority over
human society. Cicero, a favorite classical author, regards
piety as essential to virtue and sometimes writes with
religious fervor. We seek in vain for any genuine secularism among political writers before the Renaissance. Even
the most daring defenders of rulers who were in conflict
with the popes—such as the so-called Anonymous of York
(apparently William Bona Anima, Archbishop of Rouen[1]),
author of tractates about 1100; John of Paris (*Royal and
Papal Power,* 1302); and Marsilius of Padua (*Defender of
Peace,* 1324)—make much use of the Bible and remain
fully within the confines of Christian belief.

It was Machiavelli who first ventured to make a violent
break with this tradition. His startling book *The Prince*
(1513), departing somewhat from his earlier *Discourses
on Livy,* reflects his experience of the behavior of power-
seeking princelings and officials, to the total repudiation
of moral idealism, classical or Christian. Principles solemnly laid down by philosophers and theologians are cast
aside. To require men to leave what is done for what
ought to be done he deems ruinous. Since men have never
behaved according to the teachings of their political moni-
tors, these have merely made laws for imaginary commonwealths. The Christian call to otherworldliness has
been damaging to man's welfare in the present world.
Machiavelli exonerates and applauds the founders and defenders of states who have secured their power by fratri-
cide or massacre. A conqueror should "either caress or
extinguish" a conquered people. Machiavelli's one positive aim was the unification of Italy. No action tending
to this end, however base or cruel, was to be condemned.
The principles of Machiavelli have never been more un-
equivocally endorsed than by those who in our century
plunged the nations into devastating wars. But since his
time a Machiavellian strain has repeatedly made its ap-

pearance, and a thoroughly secularistic basis of politics has been widely assumed. Perhaps the most famous contribution to this trend was the *Leviathan* of Thomas Hobbes (1651).

Machiavelli's ominous rejection of the sanctities cherished by political writers from of old preceded the beginning of the Reformation. Yet however widely his principles were practiced by governing powers, they were not persuasive to the leading writers of his time. They were countered in notable writings of Erasmus, William Budé, and other Christian humanists. But it was the Reformers, and notably Calvin, who most vigorously reaffirmed the divine sanction and sacred responsibility of rulership.[2]

The Christian political theory of the Reformation differs in several respects from that of the Middle Ages. For one thing, the authority of the Bible was now in the foreground, and familiarity with its pages gave tone and vigor to the political as well as the strictly dogmatic concepts of the Reformers. Again, they were in general equipped with the language skills of the Renaissance and thus had a sharpened understanding of the ancient philosophers and of the church fathers. They were also completely alienated from the papacy and they consistently repudiated all claims to supernational authority that had been made in its behalf. Although they held rulers to be obligated to God and to their people, they recognized the sovereignty of civil states by the law of nature and of God. Thus they obtained a mastery of the older thought together with an emancipation from its later limitations.

RESISTANCE TO TYRANTS

Even before his conversion, young Calvin was the author of a work on political ethics, the Commentary on Seneca's *De clementia* (1532), which Quirinus Breen has characterized as "a muzzle for Machiavellianism."[3] The new affirmation of moral and religious values in politics was to be amply and earnestly set forth in his later works.

In the exigencies of the time, writers within the circle of Calvin's influence were led to stress and enlarge upon that aspect of his thought in which he countenances resistance to tyranny. Numerous learned controversial treatises against oppressive governments, reflecting Calvin's teaching but utilizing a wide range of sources, began to appear in his lifetime.

We may cite a few. John Ponet, Bishop of Winchester, in flight from Mary Tudor, published in Strasbourg his *Shorte Treatise of Politike Power* (1556)[4] arguing from the law of nature and from Scriptural examples that an oppressed people have power to depose and to punish their oppressors. Ponet treats the ephors and tribunes, cited by Calvin as "popular magistrates" for the protection of the liberties of the people, as the ancient equivalent of modern parliaments and diets, which properly have authority from the people under God to remove and punish tyrants. A similar argument is put forth by Christopher Goodman, loyal colleague of John Knox in Geneva, in *How Superior Powers Ought to Be Obeyed* (1558), where kings are said to hold power by election of the people and to be also God's lieutenants who must behave as such or suffer penalties at the hands of those charged to keep them in obedience to God's laws. A German document, the Magdeburg *Bekenntnis* (1550), in which Lutheran ministers declared the right of resistance by the lower magistrates to an emperor who in violation of his oath seeks to destroy the liberty of his subjects, may have lent encouragement to these writers. John Knox, at any rate, was acquainted with this precious political fragment when in 1564 he was engaged in a debate with Maitland of Lethington.[5] Knox had from the first taken the same ground in relation to English and Scottish affairs. In his *Monstrous Regiment of Women* (1558) and in his later conversations with Queen Mary he had declared not only the right of the nobility to resist in defense of the people but the right of the subject to disobey where the ruler contravenes the law of God and violates his sworn promises.

The Scottish Reformation, indeed, depended for its success upon bold disobedience by nobles, ministers, and people to Mary of Guise and Mary Stuart. The most learned defender of this course of action was the humanist scholar and poet, George Buchanan, author of *The Law of Scottish Kingship* (*De jure regni apud Scotos,* 1579[6]). Though a layman, Buchanan was an exmoderator of the Assembly of the Scottish Kirk. Like many other writers of the time dealing with the limitation of royal power, Buchanan makes use of Calvin's "ephors" illustration. But this should not mark him as merely a disciple of Calvin. It is fairly certain that Calvin, Knox, and Buchanan were all at different times and places students in the classrooms of John Major, the renowned Scottish schoolman and conciliarist. In his *History of Greater Britain* (1521) and his *Disputation on the Authority of a Council* (1529), Major stoutly contended against absolute monarchy in church and nation. On historical grounds he rests authority in the people, to whom kings are responsible. Buchanan goes little beyond Major when he argues that the traditional coronation promises of the Scottish kings bind them in a covenant (*mutua pactio*) with the people, who are obligated to him only while he keeps his promises and may depose and even slay him if he proves faithless and tyrannical. Buchanan is one of the Protestant writers who exhibit a continuity between medieval resistance doctrines and those which came out of the crises of the Reformation. It is not improbable that both Knox and Calvin were more indebted to Major than superficially appears.

THE KING AND THE PEOPLE

One of the greatest of the French political writers of the sixteenth century bears an indeterminate relation to Calvinism. John Bodin, author of the laborious work *De la république* (1576), became a citizen of Geneva in his youth but soon returned to his native France. Although he was thoroughly acquainted with the work of Hotman and other Huguenot publicists, the trend of his thought is toward absolutism. This trend is nevertheless held in check by the natural relativism of his disposition and by his wide reading. When he speaks of the monarch as *legibus solutus* (loosed from the laws), he seems to refer mainly to laws of the king's own making. Like his contemporaries, he lays emphasis on the basic authority of the law of nature and of God, and he would relate forms of government to the temperament and situation of the different peoples.[7]

In Dr. Fuhrmann's lecture (Chapter 3 of this book), attention is called to a number of French Protestant writings that deal fundamentally with the limitation of kingship and affirm the sovereignty of the people. Here, as in Scotland, there is a resumption of medieval arguments. The famous little book of Calvin's friend Francis Hotman, *Franco-Gallia* (1573), in repudiating absolutism in France cites the former role of the French Estates General and views French history in the light of a mutual contract between king and people.

Hotman's argument must have sounded a note not entirely unfamiliar to his informed readers. About sixty years earlier, Claude de Seyssel, Archbishop of Turin, in the service of Louis XII, wrote *The Grand Monarchy of France*. The work represents the royal authority as subject to certain "curbs" which, if the king casts off, he becomes "a wicked, cruel and intolerable tyrant." The various estates are to have their integral character maintained, and in major matters and general legislation the king is to consult with a council drawn from notable men of all estates. Behind such arguments lay a vast tract of medieval writing and all the coronation promises and feudal compacts of well-nigh a thousand years.

The covenant principle of limited monarchy was further advanced by the *Vindiciae contra tyrannos* (1579), written in part by Philip du Plessis Mornay. (See Chapter 3 of this book.) More explicitly than in earlier treatises the sacred covenant of ruler and people here involves a covenant of both with God. The development of the "covenant theology" (from Swiss sources) in Scotland, England, and Germany is to be associated with the growing emphasis on the threefold covenant in political thought. This principle was later to find expression in Rutherford's *Lex rex* (1644), and it was the Scottish Covenanters who most tenaciously affirmed it through defeat and persecution. Their costly resistance to the later Stuart kings was a factor of no slight importance in bringing about the Revolution of 1688. In William III, England and Scotland obtained a king who had come under the influence of the Scottish Presbyterian, William Carstares, and who was solemnly pledged, according to the words emblazoned on the flag of the ship that brought him to Torbay, to "maintain the liberties of England and the Protestant religion."

More than a hundred years earlier, William III's most distinguished ancestor had affirmed the doctrine of responsible kingship and resistance to tyranny. In 1581, during the revolt of the Netherlands from Spanish rule, William of Orange issued his celebrated *Apology*. His position was that obedience to Philip II was strictly conditional on fulfillment of the king's obligation contracted under oath and that the rebelling nobles of the Netherlands, standing in the place of the ephors of Sparta, have a duty to support a good king and restrain an unfaithful one. In the Netherlands, as in Scotland, the Reformation involved an armed revolution, but the struggle was of longer duration and greater intensity.

The Protestant Netherlands was soon to become the nursery of brilliant political thinkers. There lived and wrote John Althusius, a Geneva-trained German, author of *Politics Methodically Set Forth* (*Politica methodice digesta*, 1603). This fundamental and still challenging treatise advocates a plan of government in which provision is made for maximum cooperation between rulers and people. For the defense of the people's liberties, Althusius, like many others, returns to Calvin's "ephors," who elect and censor the chief magistrate and have power to depose him. But these electors and censors are themselves elected by and from the propertied citizens, not on a basis of universal suffrage. In effect, Althusius in his aristocratic republic limits "the people" to those who from their position and property are disposed to maintain the strength of the state. In later editions he made much of the word *symbiosis* (living together) to emphasize the helpful interchange of benefits that should mark the life of all members of the commonwealth. A modern Dutch statesman and scholar, P. S. Gerbrandy, calls Althusius "a consistent pupil of the University of Geneva."[8]

Better known among Dutch political thinkers is a native son of the Netherlands whose productive years were spent abroad, chiefly in France. Of the numerous political and religious writings of Hugo Grotius, his *Right of War and Peace (De jure belli et pacis,* 1625) makes him the founder of modern international law. Although he owed much to his Calvinist background, he favored the political supporters of Arminianism; but his theological ideas were broader than the issues disputed in the Netherlands, as his once-popular book *The Truth of the Christian Religion* (1627) testifies. Central to his thought is the concept of a natural law identical with the law of God and so fixed that God himself could not change it, residing in human nature and inseparable from it. When a ruler attempts some action in defiance of this law of nature he must be disobeyed and may be deposed and even punished with death.

Later in the seventeenth century the Netherlands gave hospitality and opportunity to many Huguenots who fled thither from the persecutions of Louis XIV. Of these the learned and temperamental Pierre Jurieu was one of the most impressive writers on government. In his *Sighs of*

France Enslaved and Aspiring Toward Liberty (1689–
1690), Jurieu argues that the French monarchy was originally elective and responsible and has only by usurpation
become absolute and despotic. He advocates not a democracy but the English system, which he describes as "monarchy tempered by aristocracy." Here, as earlier, he
declares for the English Revolution of 1688 and urges a
similar movement on the part of resolute leaders in France.
A similarity has been noted between the work of Jurieu
and that of John Locke, but his recognition of religious
liberty is more restricted than Locke's. When resistance
to the suppression of the Reformed religion in France
took the form of armed revolt in the Cevennes (1702–
1711), Jurieu urged English intervention in behalf of the
religious rebels (the Camisards), and in various tracts
added new contributions to the theme of limited monarchy and resistance to oppression.[9]

Jurieu's political ideas represent a revival of the type of
thought of the sixteenth-century Huguenots. During the
early seventeenth century, French Protestants, enjoying
the benefits of the Edict of Nantes (1598), began to take
a more favorable view of the monarchy than their predecessors had done in the era of struggle and persecution.
Even after the Edict was freely violated, in a vain attempt
to conciliate the king and gain some relief from oppression
many of them voiced the doctrines of absolutism. But
when their hopes were finally dashed by the revocation of
the Edict and the accompanying active measures of suppression, they reverted to political patterns more typical
of Calvinism and assailed the absolute monarchy with
learning and passion.

The eighteenth century was everywhere productive of
thinkers who laid primary emphasis on nature and natural
law. One of those who commanded most attention in
political thought was Jean Jacques Burlamaqui, professor
of ethics and law in Geneva, whose forebears had narrowly
escaped death in the St. Bartholomew Massacre. His

Principles of Natural and Political Law (1747), widely circulated in many languages, helped to lay the basis of the American doctrine of the rights of man. He held that God's purpose in creating man was "to render him happy," and the natural right to "the pursuit of happiness" is a basic element in his political philosophy.[10] Both Burlamaqui and John Jacques Rousseau were natives of Geneva, a fact that does not necessarily make them Calvinists. Rousseau praised Calvin for his part in framing the laws of Geneva, and no doubt his *Social Contract* (1762) bears traces of the influence of numerous writers nearer than he to the Calvinist tradition. In this work he describes Christianity in something like Calvinist terms, but regards it as producing an excessive resignation inconsistent with political action. His conception of government involves absolutism without a king. One may think of these writers as tangential to Calvinism, though somewhat indebted to it.

NAMES TO REMEMBER

It was unavoidable that only a very limited number of the political thinkers of Reformed and Presbyterian affiliation could be brought under review in this volume. The company could be doubled without much loss of quality if practical statesmen, not concerned to expound their theories, had been admitted. Though we may regard Lincoln as primarily one of the doers rather than of the thinkers, we are not in doubt that his thoughts were worthy of his deeds. The same may be said with some justification of many others, some of them more closely related to historic Calvinism than he. Hungary in the early seventeenth century had the liberators Stephen Bocskay (d. 1606) and the devout soldier Gabriel Bethlen (d. 1629). Oliver Cromwell, a Calvinist who detested Presbyterians, a personality too many-sided to be classified here, having felt obliged to bring about the death of a king, ended his career as a frustrated dictator (1658). John De Witt, Grand Pensionary of Holland and policy maker of the Dutch Republic through nineteen perilous years, was a consistent advocate of government "by an assembly elected by the people." He so dreaded a monarchical trend that he long prevented the appointment of a stadtholder of the House of Orange, marshaling Scriptural arguments for his resistance. He met death at the hands of an angry mob in 1672. In France, Henry IV's able minister, Maximilien de Sully, remained steadfastly Protestant while approving the king's prudence in turning to the Roman Church to gain the peace of France. Sully gave distinguished service toward the restoration of the French state through Henry's reign (1593–1610). He later recorded, and may have originated, Henry's "Grand Design" for a Christian commonwealth comprising fifteen powers of Europe to be ruled by a general council, though we may note in passing that there were ruthless features of this grandiose scheme by which the world was ultimately to be reduced to the control of a European federation in which France would play the leading role. Incidentally, we may here remind ourselves that the Quaker William Penn, author of a more ethical project of unification, *Essay Towards the Present and Future Peace of Europe* (1693), spent some years of his youth as a student in the Huguenot academy of Saumur, where the highly gifted theologian Moïse Amyraut presided and taught.

After 1685 a politically crushed remnant of Protestants survived in France to the Revolution, religiously served by the hunted "Pastors of the Desert." A very active leader of this company was Paul Rabaut, who was largely instrumental in gaining for Protestants the measure of freedom accorded in 1787. His son, Rabaut Saint-Étienne, also a pastor, became a prominent figure in the Estates General of 1789 and a president of the Constituent Assembly. He was a Girondist who sought, not the destruction, but the assured limitation of the monarchy. Representing, as he said, two million Protestants, he called, not for toleration, but for full liberty of religion. Finally persuaded that Louis XVI must be brought to trial, Rabaut still hoped that he would be spared the death sentence. Under the Terror he was himself sent to the guillotine (1793).

Of the Protestants who rendered public service in post-revolutionary France none is more noteworthy than François Pierre Guillaume Guizot, descendant of a line of pastors and educated from early childhood in Geneva. Having published a critical French edition of Gibbon's *Decline and Fall of the Roman Empire,* he was, at twenty-four, appointed professor of history in the Sorbonne. He later held a number of government posts, including that of ambassador to London. He was the reformer of the French educational system and was premier of France from 1840 to 1848. In office, Guizot was a political conservative and a staunch supporter of the limited monarchy of Louis Philippe. Forced out of public life in the mid-century revolution, he pursued till his death (1874) the historical and literary studies for which he is now best known. A translator of Shakespeare and a voluminous writer in the field of English history, he maintained friendships in Britain and America. Among his better-known works are a discerning book *Saint Louis and Calvin* and a detailed study of Cromwell. Guizot was a layman closely attached to his church and an international figure in Reformed Protestantism.

In the history of political thought and life the roster of prominent names of men who belong in the Calvinist tradition could be greatly extended. The purpose of the above paragraphs is mainly to afford some perspective on the careers and ideas of those who receive the attention of experts in the following essays. In different accents these worthy men of Calvinism have asserted a religious motivation in political ethics. Without prejudice to those of other traditions, who could not be presented for the reader's appreciation in this book, it may be said that the persons here brought to notice represent a segment of the Christian culture in which, characteristically, political matters are received unambiguously within the realm of Christian concern and obligation.

Chapter 2
John Calvin on Civil Government
By John T. McNeill

No responsible Christian can be without concern for civil government. This follows not only from the fact that governments are obliged to take measures affecting the Christian community, but also from ethical principles inherent in original and historic Christianity. Even those Christian groups whose members are required to abstain from political activity affirm theories of the state by which such abstention is justified. Political indifference on the part of Christians is not a mark of superior piety but of defective ethics.

It is true that in our environment, where church and state have minimal intercourse, a minister may choose to keep silence on public issues without greatly exposing himself to reproach for neglect of his proper obligations. Such an option was hardly open to a Christian leader in Calvin's world, where the impact of political acts and policies on the course of church reform was constant, powerful, and inescapable. Detachment from these political stresses was unthinkable for John Calvin, the son of a law clerk, a graduate in law, a classicist familiar with the political treatises of Plato and Aristotle, Cicero and Seneca, and a man intent on reforms that were to shake the thrones of the mighty. His concentration on Biblical studies and his labor and care for the church did not eradicate his political interest but gave to it a new dimension; the magistrate became, for man's earthly order of life, a vicar of God. It need not surprise us to find that from his Commentary on Seneca's *Treatise on Clemency* of 1532 until that hour in 1564 when from his deathbed he urged the magistrates of Geneva so to rule as to "preserve this republic in its present happy condition," his writings are strewn with penetrating comments on the policies of rulers and illuminating passages on the principles of government.

I. POLITICS IN CALVIN'S CORRESPONDENCE

Let us look first at some evidence of the Reformer's interest in the politics of his own time as revealed in his letters. It would be difficult or impossible to name another eminent theologian whose correspondence is so fraught with references to contemporary political issues. The letters shed some light on his political theory; but they concern us more as proof that their writer was constantly alert to any opportunity in the posture of events to support, or to prompt, a policy favorable to the Reformation. To this end he kept himself informed on the affairs of courts, the ambitions of political personages, the strength of their following. He did not hesitate to proffer his advice to kings and statesmen even on slight chance of its being accepted. Materials of this sort in his letters have often been overlooked by readers concerned only with theological or ecclesiastical data; but they are very abundant. In rare instances the details given seem to run beyond public issues bearing on the church and to betray a certain fascination in mere shifts of politics; but the interests of the religious cause are paramount.

We can allow ourselves only a few instances. On 13th November, 1537,[1] writing to the ministers of Basel, he welcomes the "opportunity of helping the brethren" (the French evangelicals) through the treaty just made between that city and the French king. Writing to Du Tillet, 10th July, 1538, he alludes knowingly to "an affair of vast consequence." This was an agreement reached between

Francis I and Charles V, and it was to lead the way for the emperor's efforts to establish religious peace in Germany, in the course of which Calvin would attend conferences at Frankfurt, Haguenau, Worms, and Regensburg, 1539 to 1541. On 15th March, 1539, on his way to Frankfurt he sends to Farel ample information on the affairs of the emperor, on Henry VIII's suppression of a plot hatched by Cardinal Pole, and on the expected succession of Protestant Maurice to the elector George of Saxony, enemy of Luther. This letter bears greetings from Wolfgang Capito and John Sturm, his Strasbourg associates, to whom, no doubt, we may ascribe some of his store of facts. Similarly replete with information about high personages is his letter to Farel from the Regensburg conference, 28th March, 1541.

It is quite evident that Calvin took pains always to be well posted on the political news and liked to share it with his friends. Robert M. Kingdon shows that after 1555 a corps of Geneva-trained ministers in France kept supplying him with information.[2] Through other channels hard to identify, including interviews with many visitors, he continually kept up with current events.

Francis de Crue, in a study of Calvin's political activity outside of Geneva published in 1909,[3] aimed to show from the letters that Calvin was and remained "bon français," a good Frenchman and a royalist even to the point of favoring Henry II, the persecutor of Protestants. This is a somewhat exaggerated construction of Calvin's statements. It is true that his French patriotism was never extinguished. He would not have been happy to see the humiliation of his native land. But he identified the good of France with the nation's adoption of a policy favorable to church reform and hoped for a firm French alliance with Geneva, indeed with Switzerland, by which the Reformation everywhere would be strengthened. His troubled letter to Bullinger, 7th May, 1549, illustrates his attitude to Henry II in relation to his broader hopes. He

advises the Zurich leader against rejecting Henry's propo-
sals for a treaty with the Swiss, not, certainly, on the
ground of anything good in Henry, who is called "a professed enemy of Christ," but on more prudential considerations connected with the cause of the Reformation. If
"Pharaoh" is rebuffed, he may join "Antiochus," the emperor, although on the other hand the proposed pact may
relieve the woes of "our wretched brethren crushed under
that fearful tyranny" in France. Calvin soon, however, lost
hope of making such use of Henry II. On 19th August,
1550, distrusting new advances by the king to the Council
of Geneva at a moment of intensified persecution in
France, he indicates to Farel that hopes placed in Henry
are vain. "The ferocity of that beast," together with the
ravages of that "raging lion" the emperor, call forth from
Calvin the prayer that either the rage of both may be sub-
dued or else that they may, as formerly, waste their
strength in mutual conflict!

In October, 1557, following Admiral Coligny's tenacious
defense of St. Quentin against an army serving Philip II
of Spain, Calvin sent to Henry a short epistolary confession of faith; it ends with a clause on obedience to rulers
"saving the sovereign empire of God." It failed of any
effect, but in May, 1559, the French Protestant church
got itself organized in spite of Henry. In the weeks preceding Henry's violent death he was menacing Geneva.
Calvin's letters of 29th June and 1st July, 1559, complain
of his implacable cruelty. Between these dates, as Calvin
would soon learn, Montgomery's lance laid the king on
his deathbed.

When new dangers threatened Geneva from the Duke
of Savoy, Calvin again thought of France as a possible
defender. On 16th January, 1561, he wrote to Coligny
craving French aid against the duke and declaring that
such action would tend to "the public good of France."
His attitude to France should never be confused with his
opinion of the French monarchs of his time. He judged

all rulers shrewdly. It is not by accident that his Commentaries on Daniel (1561), containing perhaps Calvin's most ruthless indictment of kings in general, was dedicated to his "fellow countrymen" and "beloved brethren" in France. In his Commentary on Amos (1560), where he treats Amaziah's contemptuous speech to the prophet (Amos 7:12–13), he deplores the alliance of the pope with the government of France, Spain, and Italy. Here also he assails as blasphemous the adulation of Henry VIII as head of the church in England, recalling Bishop Stephen Gardiner's claim at Regensburg in 1541 that the king "has power to abrogate statutes and institute new rites."[4]

Although Calvin repudiates absolute monarchy, his deep respect for established government and revulsion against irresponsible revolution can always be counted on. We get evidence of this in his correspondence regarding the Conspiracy of Amboise. The Duke of Guise was now ruling France with intolerant zeal in the name of the teen-age king Francis II. The conspiracy was hatched by a headstrong leader, de la Renaudie; it resulted in a feeble outbreak in March, 1560. Renaudie had earlier approached Calvin, seeking his sanction for the effort, and had been flatly repulsed. Against Calvin's protests, about sixty Frenchmen who had become *habitants* of Geneva slipped away to join the enterprise. On this account Calvin had to explain to various correspondents his attitude to the plot. Before hearing of the defeat and death of Renaudie he wrote to John Sturm that the instigators had greatly displeased him by their rash plans (23d March, 1560). Some weeks later (11th May) he cited to Bullinger proofs of his abhorrence of the conspiracy from the first. On the same date he wrote to Peter Martyr with reference to the claim by the conspirators that they had an understanding with Condé, brother of the king of Navarre, who by law stood highest in the royal council and who was to present the Huguenot Confession to that body. On learning of this, Calvin had responded that "no single drop of blood" must be shed, lest in consequence streams of French blood should flow. There remain, it is true, some gaps in the evidence. The supposition of Henri Naef[5] that Calvin would have approved of a revolt led by Condé is hard to harmonize with Calvin's insistence that no blood be shed. Moreover, Calvin explained to Coligny (16th April, 1561) that he had refused to authorize support of Condé in an act of war; here he attributes his silence about the conspiracy to his supposition that Renaudie had been dissuaded from it by his blunt rejection of the project. Yet, as we shall see, it may be argued from his principles of political authority that in some circumstances Calvin might have been prepared to approve action against tyranny led by Condé, a lawful "inferior magistrate" with responsibility for the people.[6]

The tense and perilous situation after the Amboise incident gave Calvin much concern. During the feeble reign of Francis II, who died 5th December, 1560, the nation was in the grip of the Guise faction. Calvin was anxious to see Antoine de Bourbon, the king of Navarre, assert a claim to the regency, and was continually exasperated by that prince's vacillation. We learn from his letters to Simon Sulzer (1st October), to Bullinger (1st October, 14th October, and 4th December), and to Sturm (5th November), such facts as these: One of Calvin's letters had been read in the royal council; he had been "implored" by King Antoine to send Beza to him for consultation; he had been a party to Francis Hotman's slipping away from Strasbourg to Navarre for negotiation. These letters, packed as they are with political data, were intended to convey more to his informed correspondents than to any chance reader. What is clear is that he wanted Navarre to announce with surprising promptness and a show of force his legal claim to the regency of France. Calvin was convinced that this would have brought the bloodless establishment of a beneficent regime. "I never

approved of deciding our cause by violence and arms,"
he wrote on 1st October; and on 4th December, despair-
ful over "the sluggishness of that tortoise" Antoine de
Navarre, he was sure that "if our advice had been heeded,
without a drop of blood being shed, they would have
effected their purpose." He meant that the brothers,
Navarre and Condé, princes favorable to the Reformation,
would have been the masters of France.

Here we see the great theologian as author of a bold
political plan. He who framed the motto *"Prompte et
sincere in opere Domini"* was deeply distressed at the loss,
for lack of promptness, of what he felt to be a first-class
political opportunity for the Christian good of France.
He had always deplored irresponsible violence; but is
there not here a recognizable element of calculated brink-
manship? It is intriguing to suppose that if his advice had
been taken, the sanguinary French wars of religion would
have been averted; but he later must have realized more
clearly that one element which was needed for this was
lacking. This fault lay in the character of Antoine de
Bourbon, whom Calvin was later to rebuke for his moral
offenses as well as his political spinelessness.

II. His Early Short Statements on Civil Government

Calvin's interest in civil government must have begun
when he was a precocious teen-ager at the University of
Paris. There he was welcomed in the household and circle
of William Budé, the eminent humanist. Reflections of
Budé's treatises on the Pandects and on ancient coinage
(*De asse*) and of his *Instruction of the Prince* are found in
Calvin's Commentary on Seneca's *De clementia* (1532).
In that work, young Calvin accords to Budé the palm of
erudition in France and also lauds Erasmus as the orna-
ment of letters.[7] For a decade Erasmus had been the
favorite extracurricular author of Paris students, and his
Instruction of the Christian Prince[8] stands, along with

Budé's work but with more emphasis on Christian motives, in marked contrast to Machiavelli's earlier *Il Principe,* that landmark in the secularization of politics. Calvin's Commentary may be placed in the same sequence.[9] His primary debt, however, is not to these brilliant contemporaries but to his author, Seneca; to Cicero, that "pillar of Roman philosophy and eloquence" whom he rates above Seneca for political wisdom; and to other major classical writers. Of Calvin's debt to the ancients, Imbart de la Tour remarks that "his gratitude was not servitude,"[10] and certainly the statement applies to his favorite living writers.

In this early work Calvin is the model Christian humanist. He reinforces Seneca's commendation of clemency and humanity in government by employing Christian elements at variance from the Stoic philosopher's presuppositions, as when he makes a place for *misericordia,* compassion, declaring it to be among the virtues. Seneca's belief in providence is supported by Rom. 13:1, "the powers that be are ordained of God." The ruler is warned against flattering evil counselors and against acts of cruelty that both provoke revenge and are in themselves "horrible, detestable and accursed." There is nothing in the whole book to suggest that the author has joined the company of the evangelicals or that he has their cause at heart. He is a pleader for humanity. There is, nevertheless, a continuity between the political doctrines of the Commentary and those of the mature Reformer. We are already dealing with a very earnest mind that cannot for a moment consider the political life in terms of a mere success game. The appreciation of firm and stable government, the cautious conservatism that insists on obedience, the distrust of popular political judgments, are features of his thought here not less than of his latest writings.

But after his conversion the status of public office is enhanced by the religious interpretation given to it. The first edition of the *Institutes* (1536) contains (ch. vi) most of the text of the chapter on civil government in the final edition 1559 (Book IV, ch. xx). Rulers are now "God's deputies" and their office is a "holy ministry." These concepts are well expressed in the first official documents of his reforms in Geneva. The short confession of faith, jointly prepared by Calvin and Farel in November, 1536, in the section entitled "Magistrates" has these sentences:

We hold the supremacy and dominion of kings and princes, as also of other magistrates and officers, to be a holy thing *(une chose sainte)* and a good ordinance of God. And since in performing their office they serve God and follow a Christian vocation, whether in defending the afflicted and innocent, or in correcting and punishing the malice of the perverse, we on our part also ought to accord them honor and reverence. . . . In sum, we ought to regard them as vicars and lieutenants of God, whom one cannot resist without resisting God himself; and their office a sacred commission from God. . . . Hence we hold that all Christians are bound to pray God for the prosperity of the superiors and lords of the country where they live, to obey the statutes and ordinances which do not contravene the commandments of God, to promote welfare, peace and public good. . . . On the other hand we declare that all those who conduct themselves unfaithfully towards their superiors, and have not a right concern for the public good of the country where they live, demonstrate thereby their infidelity towards God.[11]

In a similar but ampler passage in Calvin's *Instruction and Confession of Faith* (1537), obedience even to tyrannical rulers is expressly enjoined "until we be freed from their yoke." Here, however, stress is also laid on the solemn obligations of rulers. They must do nothing unworthy of their office as ministers and lieutenants of God, and they must maintain religion in its purity and by good laws guide the life of their subjects and secure their welfare. Obedience to superiors is very explicitly restricted by the prior obligation of obedience to God.[12]

In these early brief formulations we have Calvin's basic convictions about government. The same notions keep threading their way through his weightier writings. For Calvin, firm government is a matter of prime importance. It is an agency of God's sovereign purpose and it is indispensable for man's peaceable existence. For ruler and ruled "the public good" (a Ciceronian phrase) is placed within religious obligation, and obedience to rulers is emphatically limited by the primary obedience to God.

III. Points of Emphasis in the Commentaries and the Institutes

Calvin's political thinking may be followed through many passages of his Commentaries. His earliest Biblical commentary was on Romans, which has a *locus classicus* for obedience to rulers, Rom. 13:1–8.[13] He here presses the theme that magistrates are to be obeyed because they are constituted by ordination of God. To despise their power is to offend God, the author of the *jus politicum,* the civil state. Pestilence, famine, and war are sent as divine punishments, but magistrates are appointed for the just and lawful government of the world. He goes on to argue from vs. 3 and 4 for obedience on "grounds of utility." God's design in human government is the security of the good and the restraint of the wicked. The state is a provision for the safety of mankind, and to disobey the ruler is "to avow ourselves public enemies of the human race." The magistrate enables us to enjoy peace, and obedience to him is to be referred to the law of love. Christian and philosophical principles are mingled in his argument. You will obey "if you wish the good to prosper, and not to wish this would be inhuman." But the obligation is mutual. Magistrates are "responsible to God and to men," and their ministry has reference to their subjects. It is stressed here and elsewhere by Calvin that public revenues remain public property and are not to be iniquitously spent for private luxury (on Rom. 13:6–8)

Indeed, Calvin's social and political thought is shot through with the concept of mutuality in service and in obedience. It is impossible to give here an adequate illustration of this; fortunately the topic has been amply treated by Ronald S. Wallace,[14] who furnishes scores of quotations from the Commentaries and the Sermons. "God has bound us so closely one to another that no one ought to exempt himself from subjection, and wherever love reigns there is mutual servitude," he writes on Eph. 5:21; and on I Peter 5:5: "For when authority is accorded to the aged no right or license is given them to shake off the bridle, but they also are brought into order, that there may be a mutual subjection (*ut mutua sit subjectio*)." It will be recalled that St. Benedict in his Rule for Monks (ch. 71) observed that monks are mutually to obey each other and that this is one of the chief means of grace. But rarely after the New Testament was this doctrine affirmed with the insistence found in Calvin. Ideally civil government should always exhibit this character. We shall see that Calvin also has advice for the subject where the ruler is not to be reached by Christian admonition.

Wilhelm Niesel is an eminent Calvin scholar, but I am unable to follow him when he states that Calvin is concerned with the civil power only for its relation to our fellowship with Christ and so "is not concerned about the state as such, not even about the Christian state."[15] It seems clear to me that Calvin is also interested in the civil power as necessary to the public good, the safety, decency, and peaceable behavior of mankind. One of his more comprehensive brief statements on the functions of government is found in the *Institutes*, IV. xx. 2. Here, after differentiating spiritual and civil government, he adds:

For civil government has as its appointed end, so long as we live among men, to cherish and protect the outward worship of God, to defend sound doctrine and the position of the church, to adjust our life to the society of men, to form our social behaviour to civil righteousness, to reconcile us with one another, and to promote general peace and tranquility.

If we cut this statement off in the middle, we mutilate Calvin's doctrine of the state into a shape contrary to his clear intention. In the next paragraph he castigates the "outrageous barbarity" of those who would abolish civil government, since:

> Its function among men is no less than that of bread, water, sun and air, but more honorable in that it prevents idolatry and blasphemy and provides that each man may keep his property safe and sound (*ut sum cuique salvum sit et incolume*), that men may carry on blameless intercourse among themselves; that honesty and modesty may be preserved. . . . In short that a public manifestation of religion may exist among Christians and humanity may be maintained among men.

The state then benefits Christians and other men. This does not call in question the priority of the church, the communion of saints. But Calvin the humanist survives in Calvin the theologian, and we see here the influence of Cicero[16] and other ancient writers. He elsewhere uses the 101st Psalm (which Luther once called David's Mirror of Princes) to argue that rulers are "ordained protectors of public innocence, modesty, decency and tranquility" whose "sole endeavor should be to provide for the common safety and peace of all." To this end they are vested with coercive power, to be exercised under God's authority and with that clemency which Seneca called the chief gift of princes. They have authority in the last resort to wage war for the sake of their people against rebels and invaders, and to levy taxes, remembering always that their revenues are the people's treasuries, indeed their very blood, to be used for public necessities and not to be tyrannically extorted or prodigally squandered.[17]

IV. FORMS OF GOVERNMENT

The habitual reference by Calvin to the divine basis of government gives color to the use of such terms as "theocracy," "bibliocracy," "christocracy" by some writers who describe his ideal of a political society as well as the disciplined community of Geneva under his sway. That such terms have been proposed as keys to his political intention is itself significant. But they are not free from ambiguity and are not very helpful toward an understanding of his mind or his Geneva. If "theocracy" is taken in its popular sense of hierocracy, government by priests, rather than in its basic meaning, government by God, it is an inappropriate way to describe the situation at Geneva, for there Calvin separates the magistrate from the clergy. He and his ministerial associates held no political offices or magisterial authority in Geneva. If "bibliocracy" means a government based on Biblical principles, it is vaguely applicable; but not if it implies a basis of Biblical legislation. The notion that a modern state must not be "ruled by the common laws of nations" but in accordance with "the political system of Moses" Calvin explicitly rejects as "seditious, false, and foolish."[18] The eminent visitor who saw in Calvin's Geneva "the most perfect school of Christ"[19] might have been willing to apply the term "Christocracy" in this connection. And Calvin's statement that "kings and princes should not think it a disgrace to them to prostrate themselves suppliantly before Christ, the King of Kings"[20] has many parallels in his writings. But the term is not comprehensive enough. His political thought ranges beyond Christian governments. In areas where Christ's kingship is not thought of by ruler or people he sees the civic order as a valid organ of the divine purpose functioning through natural law.[21] André Biéler has recently written:

The question whether the magistrates must personally be Christians is fundamentally not very important. Calvin wanted them to be so. But in his encouragements to the persecuted churches he well demonstrated that the obedience of Christians to the magistrates is by no means conditioned by the faith or by the lack of faith of these authorities.[22]

Obedience, and the limitations of obedience, do not differ by reason of the ruler's religion; the issue arises, rather, where he commands what God forbids.

Calvin did not draw up a utopian scheme of government and he is content to be somewhat inexplicit with regard to the ideal structure of the state. In general, he views any existing government as a thing given and not to be called in question. He often ranges kings, magistrates, and other officers indifferently, as alike God-ordained and so to be revered and obeyed and as alike responsible for the public good. He was, of course, familiar with the treatment of forms of government by ancient writers and like them he was well aware that good government is not automatically assured through the adoption of any one of these. "It is not easy," he confesses, "to distinguish which one of them excels in usefulness."[23] We are not justified in tagging him with a label that would identify him with any modern political school. To his cultured despisers on the left his stress on obedience has made him a political and social reactionary, whereas to those on the right his espousal of the freedom and welfare of the people marks him as a dangerous revolutionary. His partisans, in turn, have tended to find in his pages support for their own political preferences, or even their own political indifference. The passage in which he briefly but explicitly compares monarchy, aristocracy, and democracy reflects the commonplaces of the Greek philosophers.[24] Each form has its typical perversions. Kingship may lapse into tyranny, aristocracy into the faction of a few, and still more readily, the rule of the people into sedition. This much Calvin and his contemporaries learned from Plato, Aristotle, and Cicero. A few years earlier Zwingli had similarly stated the matter with the declaration that "we must be alert" to prevent such deterioration.[25] But Calvin had an afterthought that must be held to cancel his seeming indifference to forms of government. When settled in Geneva, in the 1543 edition of the *Institutes* he introduced into this paragraph a frank statement of preference:

For if the three forms of government which the philosophers discuss be considered in themselves, I will not deny that aristocracy, or a system compounded of aristocracy and democracy (vel aristocratian vel temperatum ex ipsa et politia statum) far excels all others.[26]

And what is aristocracy in Calvin's vocabulary? The whole passage shows that the words of Greek origin used in it are used in their classical sense. For Plato aristocracy is "government by the best," the rule of "the truly good and just man."[27] For Aristotle it is "the distribution of honors according to virtue (aretē)," since "virtue is the defining factor of aristocracy, as wealth is of oligarchy and freedom of democracy."[28] Once in this context Calvin uses Cicero's word "optimates" for the best men, a word which historically sometimes stood for members of the best families, but is apparently here employed in innocence of such implication. Now he does not tell us here how the excellent men become magistrates. But it may be significant that the phrase "compounded of aristocracy and democracy" was set into the Institutes in the year in which Calvin participated in the revision of the constitution of Geneva.[29] By this constitution the four syndics who were the chief magistrates of the city were elected by the General Council of all citizens, but they were not nominated by it. A list of eight names was prepared by the Little Council and presented to the General Council which by vote elected four of the eight. As for the Little Council, it filled its ranks by co-optation, subject to the approval of the Council of Two Hundred, whose membership was also nominated by the Little Council. This is "aristocracy compounded with democracy," Geneva style. Essentially it existed before Calvin's time but it was retouched by him. It is an aristocracy of excellence, not of lineage, checked by the democracy of popular election. The "best men" are chosen by popular vote from a restricted list of names selected by their experienced predecessors in office.

The system illustrates a principle that Calvin was to

state more explicitly by another insertion in the same section in his 1559 edition. Here he explains his preference for the aristocracy-democracy type of government on the ground that kings actually lack that self-control, discernment of justice, acumen, and prudence needed for sound government, so that "it is safer and more bearable for a number to exercise government" (*ut tutius sit ac magis tolerabile plures tenere gubernacula*) "so that they may help, teach and admonish one another; and if one asserts himself unfairly there may be a number to restrain his wilfulness." Calvin finds this model regimen in Ex., ch. 18, and Deut., ch. 1, and declares most happily that government in which "freedom is regulated with becoming moderation and is properly established on a durable basis." Where such freedom exists, magistrates are to be alert and careful to preserve it; else they are "faithless men, and traitors to their country."[30] With this important passage may be linked his statement of the same period that kingship by hereditary right seems not to be in accord with liberty and that a well-ordered government is derived from the general vote of the people.[31] But basically it is perhaps not the fact of hereditary succession that repels Calvin so much as the assumption that one mortal man, by his own talents and with no one to say him nay, is competent to meet the responsibilities of government. Where high decisions are made he finds safety in plurality (*plures*) and in the consequent opportunity of mutual admonition and the pooling of wisdom. And even the "best men" have to pass the test of the ballot box.

V. RESISTANCE TO TYRANNY

Much has been written about resistance to tyranny as a significant element of Calvin's political thought. Its significance is hardly lessened by the fact that it received scant space in his writings. For his conservative mind it was difficult to make a place for any resistance by sub-

jects even to the most oppressive ruler. Yet the topic
creeps into some of his commentaries and is given remarkable prominence in the closing paragraphs of the
Institutes. We must submit, says Calvin, meanwhile im-
ploring the help of God. But as Israel was delivered from
the tyranny of Pharaoh through Moses and later sometimes chastised by foreign enemies who were unwittingly
acting as agents of the divine will, so God by such means
"breaks the bloody scepters of arrogant kings" and "over-
turns intolerable governments." The obvious inference is
that we are to acquiesce in revolutions in which oppressive regimes are overthrown. Audaciously, Calvin adds:
"*Audeant principes et terreantur,* Let princes hear and be
afraid!" These words are in every edition of the *Institutes*.
In the first edition they must have been consciously flung
back by the young exile at King Francis I under whom
Calvin's friends were being tortured and burned.

He notes, moreover, in some states the existence of
"magistrates of the people (*magistratus populares*)"[32]
whose function it is to check the despotism and licentious-
ness of kings. Such were the ephors of Sparta, the tribunes
of Rome, and the demarchs of Athens, and "perhaps,"
he adds with seeming casualness, "the three estates of
modern realms."[33] These magistracies are by God's ordinance protectors of the freedom of the people, and it is
nefarious perfidy on their part to wink at royal oppression
of the common folk. Here too, as often elsewhere, Calvin
reminds his readers that there is always one reservation
to be observed in connection with the obligation of
political obedience; the prior requirement is obedience to
God.[34] Two years after the last Latin edition of the *Institutes,* commenting on Dan. 6:22, "Before thee, O King,
I have done no hurt," he observes:

For earthly princes lay aside their power when they rise up
against God, and are unworthy to be reckoned among the
number of mankind. We ought rather utterly to defy them

[*conspuere in ipsorum capita*, literally, to spit on their very heads] than to obey them.[35]

This is rough language even for a fighting theologian: its tone reveals Calvin's perturbation over the untoward events of 1561.

In seizing upon the ephors and tribunes of antiquity for his argument on the restraining power of popular magistrates, Calvin may have been indebted to Zwingli,[36] who, however, omits the demarchs and applies the reference to the authority, not of magistrates, but of pastors. But the argument grows out of Calvin's whole structure of thought. It is consistent with his constant rejection of any right vested in the private citizen to resist his ruler. We are to wait until intolerable government is overturned either by God's use of the wrath of men or by action of the constitutional defenders of liberty. It is consistent with his attitude to the Conspiracy of Amboise, whose leader he judged, not one of those *magistratus populares* who were appointed to withstand royal oppression, but a political hothead, unauthorized and irresponsible. It is true that where no constitutional defenders of the people's liberty exist in a state Calvin gives no lead for possible resistance. But he must have known that nearly all European states had developed and were employing some organs of representation and more or less effective checks on absolutism, though in his native France the meeting of the Estates was only a memory and a hope. After his death, Calvin's more aggressive friend Francis Hotman, and more than a century later the Huguenot writer Pierre Jurieu, were among the strong advocates of the power of the Estates as over against that of the king; and the tradition reaches to the revolutionary Estates General of 1789. The "ephors" passage became a commonplace of Reformed political writing for generations. Calvin's single sentence of 88 Latin words proved more impressive, perhaps even more influential, than his countless warnings against disobedience.

VI. CHURCH AND STATE DIFFERENTIATED AND ASSOCIATED

Something of Calvin's conception of the relation of church and state has been implied in what has been said above. He had in mind a constantly intimate interaction between the two as partners in service to the people's needs. The picture, familiar to us, of a human community broken up for worship into uncounted fragments, all without direct relations with the government, would have startled him like a nightmare. The community of Geneva, before Calvin first saw the place, had voted for the Reformation in an orderly meeting of the citizens held in the Cathedral. Even Calvin's opponents who wanted a relaxation of the discipline were not thinking of a tolerated plurality of religious communions. It was assumed that a united church and a unitary state would jointly serve the religious and temporal needs of all the people. A generation later Richard Hooker wrote the well remembered words: "There is not any man of the Church of England but the same man is also a member of the commonwealth; nor any member of the commonwealth which is not also of the Church of England." The situation in Calvin's Geneva corresponded to this model more closely than did that of Hooker's England. It was understood that the citizens were worshipers and disciplined members in one church.

Calvin separated in thought the two entities, church and state, but assumed and provided for their mutual interaction. For him any real alienation between them would have spelled disaster. The Ecclesiastical Ordinances by which the church was governed were ratified, with some alterations from Calvin's draft, by the magistrates. Ministers were sworn to maintain the Ordinances "as approved by the councils of the city," and "to serve the seigneury and the people," saving only their service to God. The elders, who were to admonish the erring and "enjoin fraternal corrections," were already members of the elected magistracy and were nominated by the Little Council. Names were screened in a meeting of this Council with the ministers and presented to the Council of Two Hundred for approval. The election of deacons and of workers in the hospital for the aged, sick, and poor followed the same plan. Matrimonial cases in law were declared to be a matter for the magistrates, who might at their discretion call in ministers for advice. With this intimate partnership went the insistence by Calvin that the Sacraments and preaching were the undivided function of the ministers. Calvin was very sensitive to any encroachment on the freedom of the pulpit, defending this even when, as in the case of Michael Cop's sermon against Abel Pupin's play, he did not agree with the preacher. And he took a firm stand against the alienation of church property on the ground that "what has once been devoted to Christ and the Church is not the property of the civil magistrate"; the ruler has power to administer it faithfully but never to secularize it and so profane what is sacred.[37] Education of the young was one of Calvin's main concerns. Although the interest of all citizens was sought in this, Calvin and his ministerial colleagues took the lead. He was the author of the Geneva school system and of the statutes of the Academy of Geneva, which soon became an international school of great distinction. Its students were, in Calvin's words, to prepare "for the ministry as well as for civil government," and the teachers had to have the approval of the ministers as well as of the Council. In striking contrast with present-day tax-supported schools of America, the teaching schedule was marked by the intensive study of classical languages and literatures and by the apportionment of much time for prayer and psalm-singing.

VII. ENDURING VALUE OF CALVIN'S POLITICAL INSIGHTS

The highly gifted Reformer of Geneva died four hundred years ago, in 1564. But he has come to life for many readers in our own generation. Has he any wisdom for civil government from which, in our vastly different conditions, we may profit today?

Obviously we are forbidden by our total political situation from imitating the church-state complex of Calvin's Geneva. His contribution to us, if any, is mainly in the realm of principles. May I attempt to list a few points where I think we may find helpful suggestions in his teachings?

1. Calvin sets the example of a positive attitude to government and a deep appreciation of the ruler's office. He holds that for the Christian the business of government is not something alien or negligible. The state is a divinely given boon for man's safety and peace, and political activity is a realm of Christian duty. For all who in any sense stand in the Calvinian tradition this is a legacy not to be cast aside. Have we not here a lesson and an example by which we may become more effective Christians? Indeed, Calvin's teaching in this field would seem worthy of attention by all our contemporaries as the testimony of a singularly perceptive mind keenly aware of the political world while primarily concerned for the church and Christian truth.

2. It is worth keeping in remembrance that for Calvin the aim of government is the public good, conceived in the broad sense of service to every human person in his welfare, his education, his opportunity to inherit the treasures of culture and religion. He values highly a dedicated faithfulness and honesty in public men, since in their calling they are instruments of God. We have something here far above the level of the political life to which, alas, we have become accustomed. One would not go idly junketing on public revenues if he reflected that

these funds are as blood drawn from the people. Nor would the citizen and voter be swayed by inducements and promises in which he, or his area, is to be the recipient of federal aid disproportionate to need.

3. Calvin is a realist in his political expectations. He sets the standards high; but he does not expect sinless perfection in political man. Monarchy, one-man rule, is called unsatisfactory because no one man has the character and the brains for such responsibility. History is on Calvin's side here. It is replete with illustrations of the misery of rule under self-glorifying despots whether set up by hereditary right or by aggressive action. There is always danger where power accumulates in the hands of one, or of too few. Authority is best exercised by constituted bodies in which a constructive mutual criticism is maintained. Let me add that a constructive mutual criticism does not mean the art of winning elections by defamation of character.

4. To paraphrase Calvin, "Let Christians hear and be afraid." Have we not been culpably negligent of efforts to set forth and inculcate high political ideals? Have we not scolded the politicians where they have offended without showing unto them a more excellent way? It has been my privilege to hear thousands of sermons. On specific and local public issues I have often heard a true note sounded. But I am afraid that I could count on the fingers of one hand any substantial pulpit utterances calculated to direct Christian thinking along the higher ranges of political service, to impart to the citizen as voter and member of society a vital sense of his general political responsibility, and to guide Christian youth looking for a worthy vocation toward a dedicated career in politics. I hope we may say that we have begun to recover lost ground here. But I believe that there has been in this century no adequate attempt on the part of the churches to confront the nations and the world with a Christian political philosophy. The *Woodrow Wilson Lectures* have

been planned I know, not merely as a means of recovering a proud tradition, but also in order to stimulate a greatly needed Christian participation in "civil government."

If in our time the realm of politics is to be redeemed from corruption and triviality and snarling partisanship, the church has a function to perform that it has too much neglected. It will not be a waste of time to sit for a while at Calvin's feet.

Chapter 3
Philip Mornay and the Huguenot Challenge to Absolutism
By Paul T. Fuhrmann

I. THE CONSEQUENCES OF THE ST. BARTHOLOMEW MASSACRE

Philip Mornay,[1] a second-generation French Protestant leader, entered the scene at the Massacre of St. Bartholomew, 24th August, 1572, in which unnumbered thousands of Protestants in Paris were surprised in bed and done away with. The carnage continued for three weeks in the capital and spread through the provinces of France. This event caused the Huguenot party to change its attitude toward the monarchy. The Crown had been so far respected by the Huguenots, but it now tried to justify the Massacre and gave contradictory versions of the happening. Hence it lost its prestige among Calvinists, who openly came to attack the monarchy with a whole series of political pamphlets and treatises.

Let us examine the principal works and then try to gather their theory of government. The most important of them was the *Franco-Gallia* in 1573 of the brilliant Huguenot jurist, Francis Hotman, whose theory was dictated by events. In his work Hotman vehemently opposes the tendencies of royal absolutism and its lawyers. He knows history and comparative law, and uses a new method. He affirms that since Gaulish times the royal power in France has been subordinated to the Estates General. This assembly in reality represents three classes (states):

the clergy, the nobility, and the towns' *bourgeoisie,* or middle class. For Hotman, however, this assembly represents the nation and holds the sovereignty. People ought always to present, through officers and nobles, their grievances to the States General, which must also decide the great political questions, such as the election of the king. The States General may try to depose a sovereign. The role of the nobility is to be a pivot between the people and the king. The king ought to represent action and wisdom. He ought not to fall prisoner to bureaucracy. He ought to be the head, but the head is distinct from the body, which is the nation. If the king disappears, goes insane, or is made a prisoner, the kingdom remains. The king has legitimate sovereignty only when his will agrees with the will of the kingdom. His decisions are valid only in a sphere limited by law. The *Franco-Gallia* was translated into English in 1721 and presented by Lord Molesworth as the best justification of the constitutional regime.[2]

We next find *The Alarm-clock (Réveille-matin) of Frenchmen and Their Neighbors* (1573–1574). This anonymous work offers a pell-mell of Huguenot political ideas after the St. Bartholomew Massacre. An analogy is made with the high priest of ancient Israel who in the name of God stipulated a pact between God, the king, and the people, the sovereign promising to rule according to God, and Israel to obey according to God. If a party did not keep his promise, the pact was void. This book states that similarly "the people may free itself from its tyrants" and that "any prescription against the rights of the people is invalid." The work appealed not only to Frenchmen who still had "some nobility of heart" but also to foreign brothers who were to come to free French Protestants from tyranny.[3]

The treatise *Of the Rights of Magistrates Upon Their Subjects* was really a course given in Geneva by Theodore Beza and published in 1575. In it the successor of Calvin under the pressure of events departs from Calvin. According to Beza, magistrates may exact submission from their subjects only in the measure in which the magistrates keep the law of God. "Manifest" tyrants ought to be punished. The States General has the right to depose a tyrant.[4]

In 1579 appeared the *Vindication of Liberty Against Tyrants* (*Vindiciae contra tyrannos*). The word *vindiciae* is a Roman term of law, meaning the thing for the possession of which a suit is brought. As this book is attributed either entirely to Philip Mornay (who is the subject of this essay) or to a collaboration between Mornay and his friend Languet, we shall discuss it later.

All these works condemn absolutism and sponsor popular consent for government. Historians in France, Germany, and Italy call these writers Monarchomachists. The word means "enemies of the monarchy" or "fighters against the king." One of their most frequent arguments is the medieval idea that "magistrates have been created for the people and not the people for the magistrates." The concept becomes, however, more exact in Beza. He writes that the purpose of the state is the order and prosperity of the social body. Hence we have here a theory of sovereignty: the people is both the final cause and the efficient cause of the authority of the king; magistrates are created by the people. The Monarchomachists insist on the idea that, even in hereditary regimes, it is the popular consent that makes the king. The *Vindiciae* says that "never was a man born with a crown on his head and the scepter in his hand." The delegation of power by the consenting people can be but conditional. From this concept is developed the contract theory. Moreover, since to God alone unconditional and unlimited obedience is due, kings are subject to the natural law of equity and to the precepts of the Word of God. We find here two different ideas converging: on the one hand, that all regimes (whatever their form) are founded on the consent of the people, and, on the other hand, as these Calvinist authors insist, that all authority comes from God. Transferred from the people to the king, the power remains of divine right; on the other hand, rebellion against tyrants is also of divine right. Following the French scholar P. Jeannin, let us examine these two contrary ideas. First, the contract theory.

The Monarchomachists use the words "contract" and "pact" (Beza's) so frequently that they are now considered the inventors of the contract theory. Their idea of contract is close to our concept of constitution. That is, the king is to take an oath to respect the fundamental laws of the kingdom. "The pact is held to express what is founded on reason and natural equity." (Beza.) The *Vindiciae* (of Mornay or Languet-Mornay) leaves no doubt in this matter, for in the Hebrew guise it distinguishes two pacts, two covenants: the first between God, the king, and the people, the other between the king and the people. God is no party in the latter pact, yet, as the two pacts are connected, God remains the voucher and warrantor of the second pact between king and people. These writers clearly make the king subject to the law. If the king breaks the law, he becomes a tyrant. But who is to judge and to say when the sovereign has broken the law? The people? No. For Beza, the subordinated magistrates, the officers of the kingdom who represent the nation, are to be the judges. The *Vindiciae* says the same: the "tutors of the people," "the ephors and public controllers"—the officers and grandees of the kingdom are to oppose a "manifest" tyrant who has broken the contract. If a man is "originally" a tyrant, that is, never has had a legitimate title, then in that case, he is just an outlaw whom anybody can withstand.

According to P. Jeannin, the theory of resistance to tyranny is the most concrete element of Monarchomachist thought. These writers constantly appeal to the people. The people, however, is to act only through its "representatives," which are the intermediary aristocracy and magistrates. And these have the right to call upon foreign powers to help them to overthrow tyrants. But, the reader will ask, what is the quorum of aristocracy and magistrates? In other words, what is the fixed number of noblemen and judges who may declare a king to be a tyrant and to depose him? Beza does not make it a question of number; he answers: the saner or sounder part (*sanior pars*). And by the sounder part he clearly means those who profess the true religion, which, of course, is Calvinism. For the *Vindiciae*, any local community (a city, a province) can take the initiative against an idolatrous tyrant, declare itself a state, establish the true religion, and fight for its defense.

We may conclude this point by saying with P. Jeannin that the Monarchomachist writings are militant works. Doctrinally they may be weak and inconsistent. Popular —that is, democratic—assertions are violent but scarce. The predominant ideal as a whole is an *aristocratic federalism* that seeks to find in the past some political forms that will favor the Huguenot minority in France. What makes the Monarchomachist treatises important is the fact that during the seventeenth century they came to be very influential in England and the Netherlands.[5] An eminent Catholic historian, E. Jarry, emphasizes that "in the *political* domain, Calvinist ideas are at the origin of the revolution which from the 18th to the 19th centuries gave birth and growth to the parliamentary democracies of Anglo-Saxon type."[6]

A consequence of the St. Bartholomew Massacre, therefore, was the Monarchomachist theories that reinforced similar concepts found in earlier English and Scottish writers such as Bracton, Fortescue, and Major, and these writers are at the root of Anglo-Saxon forms of democratic government. As for Rousseau's influence, let us not forget that, after all, he was born a Protestant and in Geneva!

II. Peace After Bloodshed

A second consequence of the Massacre was a reorganization and consolidation of Huguenot forces. They formed the Calvinist Union, which was, within the French state, a formidable republic with its general assemblies (the Synods of the Reformed Church), its provincial councils, its courts of law, its taxes, and its armies. It forced the king to recognize its legal existence (1573–1574). The Catholics, on their side, formed the Holy League (1576). The historian Michelet called this League "the counterfeit and grotesque caricature" of the Huguenot Union which alone was a true "Republic."[7]

From 1562 on, a civil war between these two forces (Catholics and Protestants) raged in France with various fortunes and terrible destruction. The armies came to be composed mostly of foreigners. We find Spanish, Italian, and Swiss soldiers in the Catholic League. The Protestants hired German foot soldiers (lansquenets) and German cavalry.[8] The most important arm was cavalry, since the war consisted principally in taking the enemy by surprise. When a town was taken, it was abandoned to pillage by the soldiery. Montluc (1499–1577), killer of Protestants in Guyenne and famous for his cruelty to Calvinists, said, "When it is a question of foreign wars a man may spare an enemy but in civil wars he recognizes neither relatives nor friends."[9] Each party saw in the other the enemy of God, whom it worshiped. The sanctity of the cause made each side forget the enormity of its crimes, rapes, assassinations. Agriculture, city life, administrative and financial structures, collapsed.[10]

The war dragged on for years and was indecisive until King Henry III of France was killed by a Catholic fanatic in 1589. Because he was the last of his family, his nearest relative and heir to the throne was Henry of Navarre, the leader of the Huguenots. But Catholics and the city of Paris would not accept him. The stalemate was solved in the way we all know: Henry gave up his profession of Protestant religion, went to Mass, and was recognized by all as the king of France. He had to grant the Edict of Nantes (1598) to his former coreligionists. Calvinists were free to worship in castles, villages, and cities where they were already established and in two additional cities for each royal jurisdiction (*baillage*). There were in France about one hundred such jurisdictions. Politically, the Huguenots were recognized as an organized body (a state within the state) with juridical guarantees (all higher courts were made up of equal numbers of Catholics and of Protestants), political guarantees (all government appointments were open to Huguenots), military guarantees (the Huguenots could remain armed and hold forts throughout the kingdom), cultural guarantees (Protestants could have colleges and universities of their own).

Thus Henry IV pacified France. His great Huguenot premier, Sully, improved agriculture and put finances in order. Of all French kings Henry IV was the most solicitous for the welfare of the common man. The qualities and abilities of Henry reerected France, and his personal influence gave her for a few years the blessing of peace and prosperity.[11]

III. THE LIFE AND WORK OF PHILIP MORNAY, 1549–1623

Throughout this long period of French history, in all this great struggle, "the most accomplished gentleman of his time, the most influential Protestant, the man who rendered the greatest services to his Church and country,"[12] was Philip Mornay, Lord of the Du Plessis-Marly domain, hence in former days also known as Duplessis. He was a fruitful writer, poet, theologian, controversialist, diplomat, negotiator, man of the sword, capable administrator, and able politician. In a time of chaos and desolation he stands out by what our forefathers called his virtues, that is, his inner powers.

Philip Mornay was born in Normandy in 1549. His mother approved of the Reformation movement and gave him Protestant tutors as well as a Latin Bible. His father was formally a Catholic but on his deathbed in 1559 refused to see a priest. The family then became officially

Reformed. Between the ages of ten and eighteen Philip read Latin, Greek, and Hebrew authors. In 1568 he decided to go to Germany. At Frankfurt (September, 1569) he came to know and to love Hubert Languet (1518–1581), who was a French diplomat in Germany and a Huguenot jurist. Languet had bold theories about freedom of thought and the people's rights versus the king's. Mornay then visited Switzerland, Italy, the Netherlands, and England. Here he addressed a poem to Queen Elizabeth recommending to her "the ruin of the anti-Christ and the re-establishment of the true Church."[13]

In July, 1572, Mornay returned to France to see Coligny, to whom he had been recommended by his friend Hubert Languet. He presented to Coligny a memoir urging a French war upon the Spaniards in the Netherlands, a memoir that Coligny transmitted to the king. During the St. Bartholomew Massacre, Mornay was a guest at the Golden Compass Inn in Paris. He first took refuge in a barn. Then, helped by his Catholic host, he took shelter in the English embassy, whence he escaped to England.[14]

Mme Mornay later narrated that while in England her husband spent his time on books, producing some apologetics of the Reformed religion in France.[15] Some historians, such as Patry,[16] think that Mornay was the author of the anonymous *Exhorting Catholics to Peace*. It states in French that the greatest curse of mankind is war, since in a few days it destroys more than other curses can in years. Even worse are civil wars and wars of religion, for they ruin not only the people, the nobility, and the clergy but also the consciences of men. The remedy for all these evils is peace.

One of the most important works is the *Vindiciae contra tyrannos* of Junius Brutus. This work was composed in 1574 in response to impressions left by the St. Bartholomew Massacre. It was published in Latin in 1579 and in French in 1581 (*On the Legitimate Power of the Prince Over the People and of the People Over the Prince*). An

English translation of the *Vindiciae* was published in 1689 and again in 1924.[17] Who is this Junius Brutus who composed the book? Its authorship was in doubt even in Mornay's time. Some historians today[18] answer that it was either Mornay or Languet without deciding which of the two. Other modern historians[19] attribute the whole *Vindiciae* to Mornay. Méaly thinks that the only serious evidence is in favor of Mornay's authorship, and he quotes the memoirs of Conrart and Mme Mornay.

Conrart says that someone asked Pastor Daillé, who lived with Mornay during the last seven years of Mornay's life, whether or not Junius Brutus (the writer of the *Vindiciae*) was Mornay. Daillé answered: "This is a question that I never dared to put to Mr. Mornay . . . but I can say that in the Saumer castle at the end of his gallery of books, he had a little cabinet containing the books composed by himself. They were all well bound. And among them was also a copy of Junius Brutus."[20] The second evidence is the memoirs of Mme Mornay relating that during a sojourn at Jamets in March, 1574, "Mornay spent his time doing some writings. Among others he made in Latin a volume entitled [in French] *On the Legitimate Power of a Prince Over His People* . . . , which has since been printed and published with only a few knowing who the author is."[21]

More recent historians[22] attribute the *Vindiciae* to a collaboration between Languet and Mornay. Its Preface suggests a collaboration of authors. It states that Brutus submitted his work to C. Superantius, who published it. Following G. T. van Ysselsteyn,[23] Patry analyzes this treatise in four parts, each answering a great question.[24] G. T. van Ysselsteyn and Patry think that the third part (given in note 24) is a treatise by itself whose content corresponds to the Latin title *Vindiciae contra tyrannos* (*A Defense Against Tyrants*). Languet is thought to have composed this third part. Parts one, two, and four are about the reciprocal attitudes of legitimate sovereigns and their subjects. These three parts are considered to be the work of Mornay.[25]

Following J. Ellul,[26] let us look at the *Vindiciae:* The purpose of this book in his view is to refute Machiavelli (the defender and sponsor of tyrants), to help the Huguenot cause, and to know that man may legitimately resist the state. The logical starting point of the author (or authors) is theocracy, that is, a God-directed state. Kings and peoples must do God's will. At the basis of all sovereignty, there is a twofold contract. The first contract is concluded between God on the one side and on the other side the king plus the people. By this contract God commands the people to obey the king and thereby establishes the right of the sovereign. The king, therefore, must lead the people according to God, but the people is allowed to revolt if the King turns away from God. From that moment the sovereign no longer has any authority. But there is a second contract between the people and the king. This contract fixes the modality of government and of obedience by the people. What is the purpose of this contract? It aims at the justice (or righteousness) of the people and of the king. The universality of popular reason will define the common good. The sovereign, therefore, may not be an absolute monarch. His authority is to be measured by his personal religion and justice. The people must constantly be represented in the face of the king on one side by the magistrates (we have Calvin's theory here) and on the other side by other bodies and the States General whose autonomy is a guarantee against the encroachments of tyrants. If the legitimate sovereign becomes unjust, magistrates must oppose him. If the occupant of power is a tyrant without legitimate title, installed by violence, then open revolt by his subjects is necessary.

The ending of the *Vindiciae* (which was certainly written by Mornay) is full of nobility and moral grandeur: "To conclude this discourse with a few words, personal

religion [*piété*] commands that we maintain the law and
the Church of God; justice wills that we tie the hands of
tyrants who ruin the law and all good government [*police*]; charity requires that we offer our hand and lift up
those who are crushed."[27]

Returning from England to France, Mornay met in 1574
in Sedan a Huguenot refugee from the St. Bartholomew
Massacre—Charlotte Arbaleste, who was a mathematician
and a painter. He became engaged to this woman of great
culture in 1575 and upon her request composed a French
Discourse on Life and Death, followed by a translation of
the letters of Seneca. The Discourse, among other works,
drew the attention of religious people to Mornay. It was
not published until 1585.[28] Consisting of meditations inspired by ancient philosophy and the church fathers, the
Discourse pictures life as a sorrowful trip through extreme
cold and extreme heat, rough mountains and precipices,
and deserts full of brigands. Death puts an end to these
tribulations and leads us to port, to our true home.

Mornay then participated in a Huguenot military campaign. He was taken prisoner, but not being recognized
as Lord Du Plessis, he was able to redeem himself for
100 *écus.* Returning to Sedan in October, 1575, he married
his dear Charlotte, January 3, 1576. Mornay then went to
Southern France. On his way he observed the terrible
devastation of war. Henry of Navarre sent him upon
several diplomatic missions to England, the Netherlands,
and France (1576–1584). Mornay first went to solicit
help from Queen Elizabeth of England, who contributed
80,000 *écus* to the French Protestant cause (1576). During this stay in England,[29] Mornay composed and dedicated to Henry of Navarre a *Treatise on the Church*
(1577), which was printed in French in London (1578).
Its Preface urges the convinced reader to profess the new
faith.[30] The book was approved as a scholarly defense of
Protestantism by the French National Synod of Vitré in
1583.

In 1578, Philip Mornay was in the Netherlands, where the proletariat and the nobility had united in the Calvinist religion in order to expel the Catholic Spaniards by means of a war that lasted eighty years (1568–1649). Mornay's mission there was to calm the passions of Protestant fanatics. He went from town to town, saying that religion ought to be preached—not forced upon people. It was not a question of compromising but of realizing that truth never resorts to violence. In this precept we find one of the characteristic traits of Mornay's personal religion: that the firmest faith is combined with unwavering tolerance. Such tolerance has its reason for being in a mystic confidence in the power of truth. Truth by itself dispels error. Here tolerance is not the result of unbelief, but is dictated by faith in the invincible power of truth.[31]

In 1580, Mornay was sent again to England to solicit help from Elizabeth, but he received nothing.[32] He returned to Southern France, where the King of Navarre decided to keep him henceforth as his personal adviser and occasional diplomatic missionary. Mornay went again in to Flanders and during a stay spent partly at Antwerp and partly at Ghent (1579–1580) he wrote *On the Truth of the Christian Religion*.[33] This is not a work of controversy with Romanism. It does not attack the Catholics or seek to justify the Reformation. Mornay clearly expresses the desire to vindicate the Christian religion above all confessions and to defend it against indifference (which dishonors Christianity), Epicureanism (which denies divine Providence), and deism (which gives equal value to all religions). This work of Mornay's was highly praised by both Catholics and Protestants.[34]

As Mornay's mission in Flanders ended, his political and diplomatic activity became intense. He set his heart upon Henry of Navarre—the Huguenots' leader who had become royal governor of the province of Guyenne—who was nevertheless a young and superficial prince. But

Mornay felt that heaven and earth were disposed toward
very great changes. "All Christendom longs for a prince,"
he wrote. "The king of France and his brother have no
children. The king of Spain is old and decadent. What a
chance is here for the king of Navarre! There is no doubt
that these opportunities are born for him, if he wills to be
born for them. Nature calls him to the French crown;
justice calls him to gather the dissipations of Spain which
does so much wrong to France." But was Henry qualified
to realize such a program? Mornay strove to make him
understand that he was destined to great things. He urged
Henry to make himself worthy, saying that Henry had
"incomparable vigor of body, grandeur of courage, dex-
terity of mind." This was the "matter" that great princes
had. All that was needed was to add the "form" to the
"matter." In other words, these natural qualities needed
to be disciplined. And Mornay devised a program to ac-
complish this: "The King of Navarre must be dressed at
eight o'clock at the latest, then call a minister to pray,
then enter his cabinet, call his advisers in council, sign
dispatches after they have been read to him."[35]

Mornay had a strong dislike for civil war but no objec-
tion to a foreign war upon Spain. He wrote to Montaigne
that the Huguenots party wanted only peace at home:[36]
"We only ward off attacks. If we are left in peace, there
will be no war."[37] But neither France nor Protestantism
could be strong and secure unless Spain was abased.
Henceforth in southwest France, Mornay watched Spain,
sought peace in France as indispensable, more and more
sought for Protestants the support of England, and sent
a report to King Henry III of France about ways and
means to reduce the power of the Spaniard.[38] Mornay
represented the king of Navarre at the Synod of La Ro-
chelle (1588), which was in reality the parliament of a
new and formidable Huguenot Republic within the old
French monarchy. This Synod of the Reformed Church
of France reorganized the Huguenot army, justice, finances, and education of youth.

As the Catholic League turned against the monarchy, King Henry III of France desired to bring about an understanding with Henry, King of Navarre. Mornay succeeded in this mediation and the two kings rewarded him with the governorship of the city of Saumur. The king of France made him a member of the French State Council. Mornay was the only Protestant member of this body. At this time Mornay hoped that the creation of a French national church council (made up of both Catholics and Huguenots) would reform the church in France and once for all settle all differences in religion according to a Formulary of the French State Council of 1590. There was the possibility of the creation of a kind of "Anglican" Church in France under the leadership of the king. The opposition of Pope Gregory XIV to this project made its execution impossible. Yet Mornay still hoped that a national council would put an end to the division between Catholics and Protestants. He even published a treatise *For the National Church Council in June 1600.* Mornay also inspired efforts to create an international Protestant Church. The French National Synod in 1614 adopted a proposal by Mornay to exclude the use of party names such as "Calvinist," "Zwinglian," and "Lutheran" and to promote an international or supernational "Christian Reformed Church." Mornay was therefore one of the founders of modern ecumenicity.[39] When Henry III of France was assassinated (August 1, 1589), Henry of Navarre was a candidate for the French throne. Because his religious affiliation was an obstacle, he gave up his Calvinist allegiance (1593) to the sorrow of Mornay, but to the joy of Mornay he became King of France.

Philip Mornay's late years were full of sorrow. His only son, serving as a volunteer in the Dutch army, was killed in a battle for liberty (1605). At the news, Mornay exclaimed, "I have no longer a son, I have therefore no longer a wife!" Mornay wrote a Latin treatise on *Tears*[40] to comfort her. In it, since he was a man of the Bible, he paraphrased passages of Scripture to bolster courage. Fif-

teen days after the son's burial, Mme Mornay indeed fell
ill. Yet she died "cheerfully, with joy and peace of conscience," in 1606, even though her last eight days were
filled with great suffering.

Mornay was to live several more years. Unfortunately,
Henry of Navarre, now Henry IV of France, was assassinated in 1610. Mornay had been governor of Saumur for
32 years (1589–1621). Perhaps this city never had a better
administration, but the new king, Louis XIII, decided to
deprive the Huguenots of this place of security. Mornay
had to retire to his estates at Forêt-sur-Sèvre. He was
always interested in the Academy (University) of Saumur, which he had organized and opened in 1599. He
was saddened by the facts that the gospel had not triumphed in France and that the Huguenots' liberties were
now precarious. He opened a temple under his roof with
Daillé as its pastor. He requested that he be buried in
La Forêt and that upon his death the remains of his wife
and son be moved in the same sepulcher. He died on
November 11, 1623, quoting the Bible in Greek and Hebrew. In one of his last moments he said that "if he had to
begin his life over again, he would take the same road,
that is, persevere in the Gospel in spite of all the disad-
vantages which he had to suffer."[41]

IV. RECAPITULATION

One hates to conclude, that is, to *close* a matter that
ought to be kept *open* and cultivated in years to come.
But one must sum up.

Early French Protestantism can be described as a re-
birth of Israel's prophetism. The movement was fluid. If
you look for true democracy in the sense of equality, you
may find it among the humble folk who first followed the
Reformed religion. Though they were burned at the stake
from 1525 on, by 1535 the movement had touched most
cities throughout France. Calvin came and organized it

into a mighty church. As for persecutions, Calvin always opposed faith to the sword. "Our patience will conquer your cruelty"—such was the watchword of Calvin and the Evangelicals of France until 1559.

In this year the Reformed Church entered the nobility, or better, the nobility entered Calvinism. Men of war, such as Condé, then Coligny, took the place of Calvin in leading Protestantism in France. These men did not conceive of government in the same way that Calvin had. Though humbling themselves before God, they raised armies, waged war on the Catholic party, negotiated treaties, resisted the king, and created a Huguenot Republic within the national state. French Calvinism was no longer a church or society of saints but a party, a Republic, a world of men and women—a new world in formation wherein pagan, Christian, medieval, and Renaissance ideas and ways of life were mixed. From these contradictions of laws and customs, from these disorders of war and hazards of life, an energetic type of man came to light. He was the Huguenot. The Huguenot was a unique combination of opposite qualities held in equilibrium: passion and reason, ardent faith and profound reflection, intense activity and voluntary self-discipline, Stoicism and Christianity.

The Huguenot was a man with a mind of his own and able to govern himself. It is important to note that only these twofold faculties of energy and control can constitute a free society and make its institutions fruitful. Calvin cannot be called a Huguenot, yet the basic virtues of the Huguenot were his. As a theology in itself, Calvinism was not really original, but what was new was its practical effect on manners and its consequences for politics. What was common to early Calvinism and to the new Huguenot world was the belief that no priest stands between God and man. The spring of religion was open to all men and women. The faithful could now freely associate in faith, in prayer, in love, and in the good life. The minister was no longer a priest but one of the brethren whose assignment was to diffuse the Word of God and to extend charity. Calvin's religion had summed this new lay world without dominating it. Some civic and political liberties were born of this religious liberty. The greatest quality of the Huguenot was indeed the ability to govern himself. And this control of self, this moral sovereignty of the person, brought about an entirely new idea and type of individual, social, and political life. We have here, not an equalitarian and flat democracy, but a varied society, hence a colorful society, hence a free society.

The year 1562 opened a forty-year civil war of religion in France which spoiled this ideal new world, arrested the spread of Protestantism in France, and killed glorious possibilities for the future. The religious war divided families, split the nation into factions, filled the century with devastations, crimes, and incredible human sufferings.

At a time when religion was too often an excuse for savage passions, when human folly was never more destructive, when all national energies were invested in crushing human beings without regard to age, sex, and social status, when humanness was degraded and the nation in ruins, we see a man standing out by his inward powers. He is Philip Mornay. He dared to become a scholar when many still considered ignorance a virtue, he was just, though a politician, he was humane, though a royal governor, he was compassionate, though a warrior, he was religious without being a fanatic. Even his Roman antagonists pronounced him "an upright man." He was a crossing of Stoicism and Christianity. His influence was great and not without reason he was nicknamed "the pope of the Huguenots."

Mornay was animated by a threefold loyalty to his: (1) God, (2) King, and (3) Country. These three great entities made the unity and greatness of his life.

1. *God.* If we analyze and compare the Monarchomachist literature we have spoken of, we can see that the

dominant principle in Mornay's thinking is always the theocratic principle, that is: God is, and to God belongs all authority on earth as well as in heaven. Everything on earth must comply with God's demands. This theocratic idea had once been used to enslave the people to kings and popes, but Mornay used it to bind people to God and to free his countrymen from perjurious kings and impious lords.[42] As a believer, Mornay was not content to reject a tradition that he thought erroneous. His faith rested on personal scrutiny and research. It was a personal ideal. His works were dictated to him by a lofty concept of truth: "Truth is strong by itself."[43] "Physical force may engender hypocrites but not Christians."[44] Truth does not need force as an ally, for "truth retains the privilege of swimming above all things."[45] This confidence in truth made him naïve at times, but never a fanatic. Mornay fought Catholicism verbally, in writing, and on the battlefield, but there is no indication that he ever used his authority to keep men from exercising the Catholic religion. The only thing Mornay feared was displeasing God. He was not so much a Huguenot as he was, first of all, a Christian.[46]

2. *King*. Mornay came to discover in the young Henry of Navarre a king according to his heart. In Henry he saw the natural king, the legitimate king, the defender of the just cause. He joined Henry at a time when Henry's fortunes were at a low ebb. He made Henry the pivot of his own policy, he influenced him, and more than anyone, contributed to place him on the throne of France. Henry IV and his Protestant premier, Sully, were the great *Messieurs* who made France.

3. *Country*. From the being of God, to whom all men owe respect, Mornay inferred civil rights and liberties. The authority of kings was limited by the authority of God. In political theory, Mornay went farther than Hotman: for Mornay, the sovereign was only the supreme delegate of the nation. Beza came out with the concept

of a contract. It was adopted by all Huguenot writers on
current public topics, but Mornay made it basic in politics: kingship was founded on a contract whose conditions
were dictated by the people.[47] Mornay completed the
ideas of Hotman and Beza, fixed some Huguenot political
concepts which passed abroad and are to be found at the
roots of our modern democracies. According to Méaly,
not all Monarchomachists had clearly perceived the principle of separation of powers, but Mornay had certainly
suspected its importance. He claimed exclusive legislative
authority for the States General and executive power for
the king. Whereas he may not have perfectly understood
this principle, Mornay caught sight of the fact that if the
legislative power is the same as the executive, there are
then no bounds to the executive power. The only safe-
guard of the liberty and security of persons is to be found
in the separation of political powers. With imposing
gravity, Mornay and the Monarchomachists set forth the
four great principles: sovereignty of the nation, political
contract, representative government, and the separation
of powers that really makes up all our modern constitutions.[48]

Though often ignored by his own nation, Mornay was
a great patriot. He wanted peace, order, and prosperity
for his native land. But he had studied, traveled, and
locally scrutinized foreign peoples and political factors in
various lands, and hence he also looked to the general
interests of Europe and supernational Protestantism.
Freed from vile passions, his meditations breathe that
sentiment of love for all men so well expressed by the
ancient word *charity*.[49] Philip Mornay was accomplished
in all possible aspects of human life. And he served the
state in the hope that the state would serve God.

Chapter 4
Samuel Rutherford: The Law and the King
By J. F. Maclear

Samuel Rutherford has had a somewhat shifting reputation. He has often been revered by Scottish writers as a saint of the covenant, a statesman of the "Second Reformation," a fit companion-in-arms of Henderson, Gillespie, and Johnston of Warriston. His English reputation, however, has been less secure. Generally, he is remembered as the author of *Lex rex* (*The Law and the King*) of 1644 and thereby as an opponent of Stuart "absolutism" and an apologist of resistance. But he is also identified as one of the Scottish agents at the Westminster Assembly, seeking to impose an alien Presbyterianism on the nation and contending for the harsh suppression of all dissent — a reputation immortalized in Milton's sonnet "On the New Forcers of Conscience."

In another area, the literature of piety, Rutherford has perhaps had his greatest influence. His warmly evangelical letters, collected during his lifetime and first published in 1664, have been reprinted several times and were especially popular with Victorians, even inspiring hymns.

All these views of Rutherford possess some truth. He *was* a Scottish patriot and churchman, a theorist of rebellion, an opponent of toleration, and a man of warm and genuine piety. And his political ideas were expressed in each of these roles and were more sharply defined because of them. It may be appropriate, then, after sketching

Rutherford's career, to discuss first his Scottish background, secondly, the themes of *Lex rex*, and thirdly, the place of this other literature in defining his thought.

I. SPOKESMAN FOR TRIUMPHANT PRESBYTERIANISM

Rutherford's life may conveniently be summarized as falling into six periods.[1] About the first, the years of preparation until his ordination in 1627, we have inadequate information. Apparently, he came from an undistinguished family in Roxburghshire in Border country and had his education at Jedburgh, the county town. From 1617 to 1621 he studied at the relatively new College in Edinburgh with such distinction that he was made regent of humanity in 1623, but an accusation of a scandalous liaison forced his retirement in 1626. He was ordained — episcopally but probably without any compromising engagement — in the following year. Now began a second period of nine years' duration, the Anwoth ministry, during which Rutherford emerged into some national prominence. His marked pastoral success, though based on genuine personal gifts, was not unassisted. Anwoth was in Galloway, strongly Protestant country and a center of the later Covenanting interest. Further, Rutherford enjoyed the influential patronage of Gordon of Kenmure, and especially of Lady Kenmure, a sister of the great Argyll and the original recipient of many of his letters of spiritual counsel. The last years at Anwoth were clouded not only by the death of wife and children but by the growing political and ecclesiastical crisis in Scotland. Rutherford's anti-Arminian *Exercitationes* (1636) and defiance of Thomas Sydserf, bishop of Galloway, after 1634, led ultimately to an appearance before the High Commission, silencing, and exile to Aberdeen in 1636. "I apprehend no less than a judgment upon Galloway," he told Lady Kenmure in farewell, "and that the Lord shall visit this whole nation for the quarrel of the Covenant."[2]

The years following 1637 were the years of Scotland's "Second Reformation," and Rutherford figured in all leading events. The eighteen months' exile in Aberdeen were improved by controversy with the "catholic" Aberdeen doctors and correspondence, spiritual and political, with Anwoth parishioners, fellow ministers, and Scottish peers.[3] The Edinburgh rising effected Rutherford's freedom, his participation in the Glasgow Assembly of 1638, his transfer to a professorship at St. Andrews, and his full emergence as spokesman for triumphant Presbyterianism, in which interest he published his second major work, *A Peaceable and Temperate Plea for Pauls Presbyterie in Scotland,* in 1642. To a colleague in these events, Robert Baillie, he seemed "godly and a prettie scholar," but immoderate.[4] Rutherford's political and ecclesiastical importance now led directly to a fourth period in his life, the London years of 1643 to 1647, his only residence outside Scotland. He joined the Westminster Assembly in joyful expectancy of English reform and religious uniformity throughout Britain, but learned to "despair of the reformation of this land, which saw never anything but the high places of their fathers, and the remnants of Babylon's pollutions."[5] Like his fellow commissioners Baillie, Gillespie, and Henderson, Rutherford not only labored in Assembly debates but preached and published industriously. Five substantial treatises date from this period.[6]

In the last two stages of Rutherford's life the tragic note deepened. By the 1650's Scottish unity was shattered, and Rutherford stood with the rigid Covenanters, opposed alike to English republicans and Scottish moderates, to religious toleration and to all political compromise designed to reach an agreement with the king. Estranged from former brethren and a leader of the intransigent Protesters, Rutherford lamented that "we took all into the covenant that offered to build with us," and that "Christ must have but a small remnant (few nobles, if any; few ministers; few professors)."[7] The Restoration disclosed the final chapter. Sick, broken by the "overthrow of the sworn Reformation," deprived of his post at St. Andrews, Rutherford awaited a treason indictment. *Lex rex* was burnt by the common hangman, but its author died in 1661 before trial.

II. THE SCOTTISH REVOLUTION

It is to the English period that *Lex rex* belongs, and it has usually been interpreted as part of the political out-pourings of the revolutionary London press. Rutherford was familiar with this swelling literature of both political camps and used or abused it in his own work. Certainly, also, *Lex rex* played some role in radical English thought and propaganda. The time of its appearance was propitious when argument, both royalist and parliamentarian, was turning from appeal to immemorial custom to more radical speculations, especially concerning the proper locus of sovereignty. *Lex rex* once again gave classic Reformed answers to questions concerning the origin of governments, the scope of their powers, popular conveyance of power by covenant, and the community's ultimate authority. Further, Rutherford's book helped familiarize the English public with pertinent Continental traditions respecting authority and rebellion, especially those of the French Monarchomachists.[8] (See the preceding essay.)

But to place *Lex rex* wholly in this context is to give it a distorted interpretation. For the treatise had a focus consciously Scottish rather than English, and its author presented it as a conservative rather than revolutionary statement. The Scottish orientation is patent throughout, from the subtitle phrase, "The Reasons and Causes of the Most Necessary Defensive Wars of the Kingdom of Scotland," to a concluding section on Scottish history and constitution. Scottish also are some of Rutherford's chief antagonists in debate, William Barclay, the Aberdeen doctors, and especially Bishop Maxwell. The same is true of many of his principal authorities — Scottish laws, cus-

toms, and confessions, and such Scottish writers as Major
and Buchanan. These references to predecessors suggest
Rutherford's related concern: he was making no radical or
original departure, but writing within an established
tradition. He saw this tradition as based partly on Scottish politics and history, partly on medieval constitutionalism, but most importantly on the heritage of the Reformed kirk.

Lex rex did indeed rest much upon Scottish political
and religious tradition, and one must look there to discover
the authentic background from which this treatise
emerged. Unlike England with its substantial inheritance
of strong central government, Scotland's monarchy had
continually struggled to establish even limited authority.
Customarily, the nobles checked the crown, sometimes
through the Estates, later through the General Assembly
(where their influence was often decisive), and frequently
through extralegal political alliances and military action.
Even in the seventeenth century the great Scottish houses
enjoyed territorial power and commanded personal loyal-
ties unknown in the southern kingdom. These practical
limitations upon the crown were strongly reinforced by
the eighty years of struggle between the Reformed church
and the monarchy. Opposed by Mary of Guise and Mary
Stuart, Reformation leaders set the pattern of looking beyond the crown to nobility and parliament as to "little
nurse-fathers." Later churchmen carried on a no less bit-
ter struggle against the Protestant but anti-Presbyterian
James VI. That king was more successful than any prede-
cessor in freeing himself from these restraints, but even
at James's death Scottish political experience remained
predominantly that of a pluralistic society with diffused
political power, suspicious of royal centralization, and
emotionally committed to the defense of "true religion"
against the political manipulations of the crown.[9]

A unique role in these political conditions was played
by the custom of banding or bonding. Of obscure foundation, though possibly related to feudal oath or family alle-

giances, banding for mutual protection or local security became common amid the disorders of medieval Scottish life. Wider use of banding to create major political alliances raised this custom to new distinction, but its most important transformation came with the great religious associations of the Reformation era. Unable to suppress the bands, the crown sometimes attempted to regularize and control the practice for its own advantage. Nonetheless, with their emphasis on shared authority, local initiative, voluntary commitment, and mutual contractual obligations, the bands were a source of political ideas and practices disturbing to monarchical power. And in this environment the covenant idea most probably had one of its origins.[10]

Scottish history provided Rutherford with valuable constitutional evidence which he might cite, but he also relied heavily on an ancient Scottish literary and intellectual tradition of limited monarchy. Medieval Scots writers, resting on a scholastic political theory that was generally European, made legitimate government serve the popular welfare and depend on the will of the community. The prince possessed only delegated power and he might be deposed. The greatest Scottish scholars at the end of the Middle Ages, Hector Boece and John Major, not only repeated such teaching but applied it specifically to Scottish history and politics, whereas the same notions in the lay poet, Sir David Lyndsay, argue for wider dissemination.[11] As modified by humanistic and French experience, this tradition of Scottish historiography and political thought was given classic exposition in George Buchanan's *De jure regni apud Scotos*. Rutherford cited these authorities, as well as the chronicles and constitutional documents that they called in witness, and there was some plausibility to Maxwell's taunt that Presbyterian political teaching went back to those who were "prior to Luther or Calvin." "Our rabbies, then have drawn these doctrines out of their polluted cisterns."[12]

The Reformation did not alter the direction of these ideas but magnified them and added to them. First, an older Scottish constitutionalism was greatly invigorated by the infusion of new religious purpose and dynamic. This was vital. We have the authority of J. N. Figgis that "it was only by adding to political reasons a religious one, that the struggle for freedom in the sixteenth and seventeenth centuries ended in any but one way." "There was one and only one motive, the religious, that could withstand the torrent of officialism, or in any way attenuate that orgy of centralisation."[13] Secondly, Scotland absorbed a Reformed political tradition which, while stressing civic obedience to authority, yet condemned unlimited power as idolatry, taught the mutual obligations of ruler and ruled, and sanctioned other forms of government than monarchy. Moreover, in Scotland the more radical interpretation of this inheritance was almost immediately invoked. Struggling against an unfriendly government, the church found Calvin's concessions to the authority of lesser rulers more appropriate to its situation than his emphasis on due submission to princes. Thus, possibly influenced by Christopher Goodman's *How Superior Powers Ought to Be Obeyed*, Knox was teaching the positive duty of rebellion against idolatrous sovereigns by 1558.[14]

A third important contribution of the Reformation appeared late in the century in the maturing of the political-religious doctrine of the covenant and its eventual association with the earlier Scottish practice of banding. The doctrine rested partly on Rhenish and English federal theology, domesticated in Scotland by the 1590's, and partly on the literature of the political contract in Continental, especially French, thought. Behind these stood medieval speculation concerning a government compact, and behind all, the Old Testament references to covenants. Although the Protestant band of 1557 has been called the first covenant, the term was not specifically applied to a political band until 1596 when the General

Assembly called for a *covenant* in opposition to James VI's indulgent policy toward the Catholic earls.[15]

Thus Scottish custom, covenant theology, and Huguenot thought conspired to complete the major political symbol of seventeenth-century Scotland. And while common in other countries, this symbol attained in Scotland a political prominence and popular appeal that was altogether unique. By the opening of that century it already was being commonly invoked to limit the king's freedom. "This solemn covenant," the ministers protested to the king's representative in 1606, "the king, and all his subjects, at his command, had renewed with God Almightie, that they should adhere constantlie to the true Reformed Religion, and established discipline of this Kirk . . . ; and let the King take to heart what befell the posteritie of King Saul, for his breake[ing] of not such an oath as the covenant of God with Scotland."[16]

Lastly, the Presbyterian movement, of which Rutherford was a committed partisan, made its unique contributions to the resistance doctrines of *Lex rex*. A fundamental reinterpretation by Prof. Gordon Donaldson has emphasized that Presbyterianism represented a late, novel, and controversial development in the Scottish Reformed kirk.[17] Owing something to Beza and Cartwright, but promoted in Scotland by Andrew Melville after 1574, Presbyterian polity required the eradication of episcopacy and the establishment of ministerial parity and conciliar government, that is, an ecclesiastical establishment practically impossible for the crown to control. It may be less certain, but still possible, that analogically this polity also suggested the value of mixed aristocracy and democracy operating under law. But most importantly, Presbyterian partisans adopted the two kingdom theory of church-state relations, already formulated in the Second Book of Discipline, by which clerical claims for the independence of the church were significantly broadened. Where Scottish Reformers, following conventional Reformation practice, had sought the rule of godly government (though locating this corporately in the Estates rather than in the crown), Melville and his followers argued for the church's perfect freedom in her own spiritual realm where the magistrate, however bound by responsibilities to the church, possessed no authority or right distinct from that of other Christians. Although this doctrine also taught the Christian magistrate's freedom from clerical dictation, its practical effect in Scotland was to promote the exclusion of the king as king from ecclesiastical decision. "Thair is twa Kings and twa Kingdomes in Scotland," went Melville's famous rebuke. "Thair is Chryst Jesus the King, and his kingdome the Kirk, whase subject King James the Saxt is, and of whase kingdome nocht a king, nor a lord, nor a heid, bot a member!"[18] Thus if an older pattern of Scottish constitutional thought endeavored to subject the king to the community of the nation, Presbyterian thought refused to have the king a "mixt person," as Rutherford said, and reduced him to a subject in the national church.

These inherited concepts of limited monarchy were finally confirmed in the Scottish revolt of 1637. The conservative character of that revolt has often been missed by confusing it with the English revolution, which began three years later. But Scottish society was unlike English society. It was less orderly and secure, but more conservative and egalitarian. It was untroubled by pressing issues of class, common law, and prerogative, or parliamentary assertiveness. The revolt began as a maneuver by nobles and kirk to preserve political and religious traditions jeopardized by the Stuarts. James VI had successfully eroded older restraints on the monarchy by confirming great families in their possession of church wealth acquired since the Reformation, thus driving a wedge between the nobility and the church, and by introducing a new ecclesiastical system based on effective episcopal administration. The policy almost succeeded. Charles I discarded the advantage through personal allegiance to a Laudian reform that not only scandalized the nation but alienated the nobility by introducing bishops as political administrators and by threatening to reendow the church with its ancient goods. The national rising was less unified and less national than has often been supposed, but it adequately replaced the forces that had blunted the power of the crown in the past. Only in one respect did the revolution suggest a fresh departure. Aristocratic leadership had dominated earlier resistance. Again this was true; but mass signing of the National Covenant promoted individualization of the covenant, more popular appropriation of constitutional convictions, and mobilization of the common man's conscience with consequences fully apparent only in the later Covenanter wars.[19]

III. The Law and the King

In the decade prior to the publication of *Lex rex,* Rutherford's actions had been consistent with these traditions. Not only had he personally defied the bishops but in 1637 he had conducted an energetic campaign from Aberdeen to win the intervention of the lords. "It is like, if ye, the gentry and nobility of this nation," he wrote to Alexander Gordon, "be 'men in the streets' (as the word speaketh) for the Lord, that He will now deliver His flock . . . ." To Cassillis: "When such a bastard and lawless pretended step-dame, as our Prelacy, is gone mad, it is your place, who are the nobles to rise and blind them." And to Loudoun: "Your Lordship wanteth not God's and man's law both, now to come to the streets for Christ."[20] Whether Rutherford had already conceived a volume that would elaborately justify such appeals is difficult to say. Perhaps the work had already been begun before attendance at the Westminster Assembly, for Baillie's letters mark Rutherford's preparation of Presbyterian defenses, but make no specific reference to *Lex rex.* In any case, the Oxford publication of *Sacro-sancta regum majes-*

tas: or the Sacred and Royal Prerogative of Christian Kings by Bishop Maxwell—a man feared in Scotland as a northern Laud—called for reply.[21] *Lex rex* appeared anonymously in October, 1644.[22]

The volume comprised nearly five hundred pages of extended answers to forty-four political queries. The work presented a somewhat scholastic appearance with divisions of questions, closely reasoned syllogisms, and copious citation of Scripture, history, and contemporary scholarship. The arguments claimed little originality, but they were framed with an eye to the contemporary crisis, and the language was bold and irreverent.

The work opened with discussion of the origins of government, asserting both God's authorship of all political authority and the people's act in initiating particular political systems. All forms of government were lawful, and all—including monarchy—were originally elective, as shown by Scotland's choice of its first king, Fergus. At this point Rutherford paused to dispose of two royalist theories, then in infancy but subsequently important—the claim that the king's title rested upon ancient conquest and the patriarchal argument.[23] But the heart of Rutherford's case lay in the doctrine of the covenant. Here *Lex rex* demonstrated familiarity with the evolution of the doctrine in Europe, both in the French religious debate and in such later critical comment as that of Arnisaeus and Grotius. Rutherford followed the *Vindiciae* of Philip Mornay in teaching three parties to the covenant—God, the ruler, and the people—and two compacts, one between God and the total community, and the other between the ruler and the people. "The Lord and the people give the crown by one and the same action; . . . seeing the people maketh him a King covenant-wise, and conditionally, so he rule according to God's Law and the people resigning their power to him for their safety . . . ; it is certain God giveth a King that same way, by that same very act of the people."[24] Should the king break the covenant with God, the political covenant is shattered and the ruler was no longer a lawful king. In such case the people "are presumed to have no King . . . and . . . to have the power in themselves, as if they had not appointed any King at all."[25] Rutherford produces historical evidence from acts of parliament, confessions of faith, coronation oaths, and custom to claim a written Scottish covenant, but he also argues that the covenant need not be written, nature and Scripture remedying the defect.[26] Finally, he insists that the people may renew the covenant without the king, if he demur, and even against his wishes, as indeed the Scots had recently done at the Tables in Edinburgh.[27]

This foundation undergirded the resistance arguments. Like Huguenot theorists, Rutherford disallowed tumult in rebellion, stressing the rightful leadership of inferior governors. These magistrates, both more natural and more necessary in society than the king, were only superficially deputies of the crown. Rather, they were ministers of God, responsible to him regardless of the king's commands, and they were to be obeyed by all as fathers in the Fifth Commandment. Inferior judges were to be found in various roles according to the constitutions of states, but in England and Scotland they were the estates of the realm. They were corporately superior to the king. Rutherford's language is extreme:

As the King is God's vassal, so is he a noble and Princely vassal to the Estates of a kingdom, because they make him. 2. They make him rather than another their noble servant. 3. They make him for themselves, and their own Godly, quiet, and honest life. 4. They, in their first election, limit him to such a way, to governe by law, and give to him so much power for their good, no more, in these four acts they are above the Prince, and so have a coercive power over him.[28]

So far Rutherford's argument seemed a fresh statement of an older constitutionalism annotated by references to Scottish history and the current British crisis. But he occasionally sounds a democratic note that undercuts these lesser rulers. He is as careful to guard against parliamentary tyranny as royal tyranny, for instance. Despite their great powers, parliaments may err, "deny their voices to things just," or "crosse the law of God." "Posterior parliaments" should correct these errors, but Rutherford also allows for legitimate popular resistance, for by their very injustice the magistrates abandon lawful office and forfeit all claim on the obedience of religious men.[29] Moreover, Rutherford expresses confidence in popular judgment as to when rebellion may lawfully take place. Royalists had argued that statecraft was complicated and that no man except the king himself could rightly judge that the covenant had been fundamentally broken. While recognizing difficulties and ruling out revolt for a few infractions of the covenant, Rutherford will have none of this reasoning. Tyranny will be obvious and the people may judge. "The people have a naturall throne of policie in their conscience to give warning, and materially sentence against the King as a Tyrant . . . . Where Tyranny is more obscure, . . . the King keepeth possession; but I deny that Tyranny can be obscure long."[30]

But does this mean that the people's pleasure is to prevail or that the will of the community is the governing consideration? No, for the people are bound in the covenant no less than the king, and the king's duty is to compel them to observe its terms. "Each may compell the other to mutuall performance."[31] Here, of course, we settle on the main theme of *Lex rex.* All rightful authority lies in law, whether it is authority of king, estates, populace, or kirk. The king is truly king only when he identifies himself with the law, and only to the degree that he succeeds in voicing and implementing law. "*Rex est lex viva, animata, loquens lex:* The king is a living, breathing, and speaking Law." His function is necessary because men naturally avoid voluntary submission to law, "so is the King the Law reduced in practice." The nearer the king personifies the law, the more king he is; "in his remotest distance from Law and Reason, he is a Tyrant."[32] Rutherford devotes no section of his work to definition of the law that the king is to incarnate. Yet he assumes that the king will serve true religion, seek the guidance of natural justice, and observe the nation's laws and customs. He quotes approvingly a Scottish coronation oath requiring the king to "maintaine the true Kirk of God, and Religion now presently professed in puritie; And to rule the People according to the Lawes and Constitutions received in the Realm; causing Justice and equitie to be ministred without partialitie."[33]

Such, in bare outline, is Rutherford's argument. *Lex rex* is not free from ambiguities, and some of these are at fundamental points. What are the terms of the covenant? Ruler and people undertake to sustain a government according to God's law, but the actual obligations incurred are never made explicit. Where in the system is Scotland's fundamental law guaranteed? Rutherford does not establish its connection with God's law, but he assumes that a constitutional violation constitutes punishable faithlessness to God. How are lesser rulers related to the covenants and how are they to be regarded as responsible representatives of the people? And do the limitations imposed on rulers primarily seek to delimit their powers or define their policies?

Perhaps too much should not be made of theoretical oversights or perplexities in *Lex rex*. Covenant doctrine served all parties in seventeenth-century controversy, royalist and Leveller as well as Presbyterian. Rutherford used it to structure convictions, religious and political, that rulers must be chained. Reformed anti-absolutist arguments once again supplied a complex of ideas by which the claims of kingship were minimized and those of the community vindicated. A theoretical heritage stressing supremacy of law, responsibility of rulers, and popular authority was restated and blended with a contemporary British preoccupation with security for Reformed Protestantism, national political institutions, and subjects' rights and privileges as established by law. This was its main work. But several additional aspects of *Lex rex* require special stress. These are not the emphases of the book, but its significant suggestions and implications. By reference to the larger context of Rutherford's history, they assume an important place in the final definition of the author's meaning.

IV. IMPLICATIONS

First, despite its bold language, *Lex rex* harbored a conservatism that, especially in England with its more varied political offerings, was recognized as a central position, serving those who reluctantly warred against the king yet desired to avoid social upheaval. For although Rutherford was determined to contain monarchy, he conceived no new constitutional machinery by which this might be achieved. He sought no republic and professed himself satisfied with a hereditary monarchy.[34] At the Restoration he wrote of his party as "gentlemen most loyal, and never . . . enemies to his Majesty's royal power; but only [they] desired that security might be had for religion and the people of God, and persons disaffected to religion and the sworn Covenant abandoned."[35] He eschewed all social radicalism and rejected the theocratic delusion. Dominion and civil power, he said, were not founded on grace, and the covenant did not "force the King to submit to Christ's Scepter" but only provided that "the Estates of Scotland have power to punish the King, if he labour to subvert Religion and Lawes."[36] Thus Rutherford's thought, although less creative than some contemporary political thinking, was also more positively related to the realities of the constitutional contest. Especially in Scotland, it strengthened popular faith in resistance doctrines, nerved opponents of the restored Stuarts, and ultimately helped frame the Whig justification for the 1688 Revolution.

Second, unlike the Leveller *Agreement of the People*, Rutherford's covenant did not attempt to secure individual

liberties. Rather, his thought supported strong government in acts of vigilance and control. The religious ruler
was pledged to fall upon subjects conceived to be in rebellion to God's law.

Third, while *Lex rex* expected the agreement of religion
and Scottish constitutionalism, religion remained the main-
spring of the system. It was from the covenant with God
that the political covenant apparently derived its force.
Further, the religious covenant operated only partly on the
constitutional plane. Primarily, it was devotional—no
measured bargain, but commitment and piety. Again,
while the political covenant was sometimes recognized as
a convenient and even necessary myth, the covenant with
God was real, historically realized in Scotland's covenants.
These themes suggest at least the possibility of a religious
yearning for a more radical conformity to God's law than
that provided by Scotland's traditional government and
law. This could prompt idealism and reform in government. It could also result in some devitalization of constitutionalism.

Did Rutherford ever make the ideas of these last two
considerations prominent? They were most likely to become so when both dangerous apostasy and intense religious excitement prevailed—as in revolutionary Britain.
Accordingly, it is possible to show Rutherford reflecting
some Scottish reactions that were to produce political
problems for the nation in the later part of the century.

First, Rutherford was the author of the most elaborate
antitoleration literature of the revolutionary age. In this
cause he petitioned the government, preached to parliament, and wrote his comprehensive treatises, *A Survey of
Spirituall Antichrist* and *A Free Disputation against Pretended Liberty of Conscience.* Rutherford carefully kept
the magistrate's labors within the limits sanctioned by the
two kingdom theory. The sword could not convert; only
ministers might labor in this field. The silent heretic was
not to be molested. Aliens, Indians, Jews, "Papists . . .

educated in Idolatry," and others without the national community were not to suffer persecution. The magistrate's work was directed, not to the punishment of the heretic, but to the kingdom's spiritual health, "the not perverting of soules and disturbing the safety of humain societies." Yet the idolater and seducer should die.[37] Rutherford knew the burning English debate on the issue and he systematically closed doors to avenues by which some Puritan writers were creatively working their way to toleration. He would have none of "Mr. Williams Chaldean, and Heathenish or American peace." The king was to "take vengeance upon blasphemy, idolatry, professed unbeleefe . . . which are ills not formally contrary to externall quietnesse, but . . . moral ills hindering men as members of the Church in their journey to life eternall . . . ."[38] Williams' typological argument was false. King Charles was burdened with the same responsibilities as the godly princes of Israel.[39] Radical Independents' trust in discussion under the guidance of the Holy Spirit could lead only to doubt and confusion.[40] John Goodwin's rationalism and exegetical refinements were paths to atheism.[41] On the eve of the Restoration he was still organizing protests against "that vast Toleration in things Religious . . . whereby the tye and obligation of these Covenants is wholly casten louse, and turned into oblivion."[42]

One must not excessively press the responsibilities of these ideas for Scotland's intolerance. Unlike England, Scotland emerged from the revolution with no substantial and enduring religious minorities to challenge church and state. And in a larger context, Scotland in the seventeenth century was struggling for unity and focus rather than freedom and diversity of ideas. But the failure to produce comparable theological bases for free religious inquiry and expression made some contribution to the greater reluctance with which Scotland abandoned political suppression of heresy and irreligion.[43]

Lastly, we distort the Scottish political outlook in Rutherford's day if we do not make some allowance for the extraordinary religious setting in which he wrote. In 1639 Rutherford addressed an epistle to the Church of Ireland. The letter is too long to reproduce, but several extracts may suggest the rapture in which it was composed:

We take them captives whose captives we were, and we rule over our oppressors. It is not brick, nor clay, nor Babel's cursed timber and stones, that is in our second temple; but our princely King Jesus is building His house all palace-work . . . .
We do welcome Ireland and England to our Well-beloved. We invite you, O daughters of Jerusalem, to come down to our Lord's garden, and seek our Well-beloved with us. . . . The kings of Tarshish, and of the isles, must bring presents to our Lord Jesus. And Britain is one of the chiefest isles; why then but we may believe that our kings of this island shall come in, and bring their glory to the New Jerusalem . . . .
Walk not in the way of those people that slander the footsteps of our royal and princely anointed King Jesus, now riding upon His white horse in Scotland. . . . That decree of Zion's deliverance, passed and sealed up before the throne, is now ripe, and shall bring forth a child, even the ruin and fall of the prelates black kingdom, and the AntiChrist's throne, in these kingdoms . . . . Who did ever hear the like of this? Before Scotland travailed, she brought forth; and before her pain came, she was delivered of a man-child.[44]

As this suggests, Rutherford's piety works a shift in the perspective from which his thought is viewed. To read his letters and sermons is to leave behind the reasoned argument of his serious works and enter a world of deep religious ardor and expectancy. Reading the signs of the times, he believed that God was at last working his miracle of history whereby Christ's kingship would be fully acknowledged by the nations. The great struggle was then in progress, Antichrist would be beaten down, and Scotland, as a new Israel, would play a glorious role in the cosmic plan.[45]

There is evidence, moreover, that this sense of Scotland's mission was common in the church. It sprang partly from national pride and partly from the view that only Scotland and Holland had produced national Reformed churches, and the heterodoxy and toleration of Amsterdam measured the apostasy of the Dutch. "Mercie and truth, righteousnes and peace," David Calderwood told his countrymen in 1620, "had never since Christs comming in the flesh a more glorious meeting . . . then ye have seene amongst your selves in the roughe end of this northern Yland: which therefore hath justlie obteined . . . a great name among the cheefe Kirkes and Kingdomes in the World."[46] And in the 1630's Rutherford, pointing to Ezekiel and Psalms, was preaching that Scotland's destiny was specifically revealed in Scripture: "Now, O Scotland, God be thanked, thy name is in the Bible. Christ spoke to us long since, ere ever we were born Christ said, 'Father, give me the ends of the earth, put in Scotland and England, with the isles-men in the great charter also.' "[47] Events in France, Germany, and Bohemia, as well as Britain, reflected the great battle's raging. By 1640 an English reformation was ripe, and Rutherford was preaching sermons of boundless joy and victory:

Who knows but this great work which is begun in Scotland now when it is going into England, and it has tane some footing there, but the Lord He will make it to go over sea? . . . Who knows but He will make [Scotland] a sharp threshing instrument to beat Rome and the Pope and Antichrist to pieces . . . . O! for to see that great stumbling-block . . . tane out of the way, and then to see the people of the Jews brought in again to Christ, their old Husband. . . . O! to see our Redeemer Christ have one fair day of it in the world; to see Jew and Gentile married on Christ and to see His dominions going from the East to the West and from sea to sea.[48]

How did this piety affect the political assumptions of Rutherford and other Scottish churchmen? Certainly, it radically deepened the determination to withstand a king whose refusal to covenant was viewed not only as evidence of tyranny but of opposition to God's providential plan for Scotland. Because we are not sure exactly what Rutherford expected history to bring forth, it is difficult to go beyond this. But at least he speculated on such an impending climax of Christ's kingly rule as might soon bring into question a political theory more appropriate to a vanishing age. One must be cautious here because *Lex rex* was itself written while Rutherford acutely experienced these hopes. But Rutherford's contemporaries sometimes expressed heightened expectations of magistrate and covenant. Was the magistrate God's minister, serving his church and law in a fallen natural world, or was he to be a Christian instrument in a miraculous renewal? Was the covenant a pact of limitations, hedging the king with constitutional and religious restrictions, or was it an offering of hearts and minds, pledging the nation to unstinted faithfulness to God's will? Constitutionalism might pale before the more radical of these alternatives. Magistrates lacking in godliness might have to be withstood, and political compromise might be impossible. If truly Christian magistrates gained the power, restraints on their power might be impiety. Rutherford avoided some of these conclusions and spoke conventionally of Christ's kingship in his church. Yet we hear him advising Loudoun to disregard the law, because "when your foot slippeth in such known ground, as is the royal prerogative of our high and most truly dread Sovereign . . . and the liberties of His house, He will hold you up." We see him denouncing Presbyterian moderates and explaining his estrangement from Dickson, Baillie, and Blair: "That Christ ought to be a King in Scotland, and the people ought to employ the liberty that Christ hath bought to them with His blood, is among fundamentals with me."[49] And while renouncing the sectarian idea of a government of saints, he held fiercely to the Act of Classes that provided a practical means whereby a genuinely godly rule was assured.

Rutherford did not act consistently in this vein. Yet these ideas supplied perplexities that were seldom absent, and Rutherford died confessing both his faith in Christ's British kingship and his agnosticism as to the means by which it would be fulfilled: "I believe He cometh quickly who will remove our darkness, and shine gloriously in the Isle of Britain, as a crowned King, either in a formally sworn covenant, or in His own glorious way; which I leave to the determination of His infinite wisdom and goodness."[50] This heritage too he left to the Covenanter Age.

V. SIGNIFICANCE FOR TODAY

What is Rutherford's significance today? He is not read, and most modern readers would find him unreadable. Even the impressive renaissance in Puritan studies that has found Goodwin and Lilburne exciting has displayed little interest in Rutherford. Yet he deserves our attention in several respects.

First, he is the best point of departure for understanding late seventeenth-century Scotland. After the Restoration the several aspects of his thought played their roles in the political struggle. Most opponents of the extreme reaction, Covenanter and Whig, used the anti-absolutist arguments.[51] In some of them, Rutherford's ideas were altered by exaggerated or partial expression. At one pole extreme Cameronians renounced allegiance to Charles II, took godly governors, and placed themselves under the sole authority of the Word. Conversely, the Scottish Claim of Right of 1689 made no reference to covenants, but otherwise echoed the constitutional assumptions of *Lex rex.*[52] Yet Scottish tradition, as it emerged into the eighteenth century, generally made allowance for both themes. Common opposition to Stuart policy eventually united political and religious dissenters in the Restoration as it had in 1637, and Sir James Steuart, Covenanter and later Whig statesman, was Rutherford's true successor in his *Jus populi vindicatum* (1669).[53]

Secondly, Rutherford helps to define the place of Scotland and of partisan Presbyterianism in the British revolutions of the seventeenth century. His restatement of the Reformed tradition was more satisfying to the Scottish than to the English revolution. The prime need of Scotland, William Haller has said, was the freedom and solidarity of the kirk as the effective organ of spiritual life in an unstable society. By contrast, England was seeking means whereby individual freedom might be assured in a stable society.[54] Liberty in Scotland was prized, but it was the liberty of men related to ranks, orders, and corporations with traditional privileges fixed by law. Such a background enabled Rutherford to combat Scottish royalists and English Laudians, but he could not appreciate the political and religious liberty conceived by Independents, sectaries, and Levellers. Even the English Presbyterians were to take a path that would have exasperated him. Baxter voiced political views much like those of *Lex rex,* but Baxter stood at the head of a tradition that led through Howe and Calamy to the Presbyterian radicalism of the eighteenth century.[55] Scottish Presbyterian adjustment to that kind of liberalism was less easily achieved.

Lastly, Rutherford's is the most notable English expression of classic Reformed political thought in the seventeenth century. By the next century he was largely forgotten, but in his own age he was linked with Buchanan as a father of orthodox doctrine.[56] Like Knox and Buchanan, he wrote at a time of national crisis, and his writing, impregnated with a new sense of Scotland's destiny, helped fix an enduring national tradition disposed to challenge oppressive government and refer political decision to moral law.[57] This indeed is how he saw the work. In the preface to *Lex rex* he gave a modest but reasonable estimate of his labor. He regarded himself as a faithful watchman. "Many before me," he confessed, "hath learnedly trodden in this path." He wrote that he "might adde a new testimony to the times." Such a new statement was needed because apostasy had "made a large step in Britain," and "Arbitrary Government had over-swelled all banks of Law."[58]

Chapter 5
The Puritan Ethic and the
Spirit of American Democracy[1]
By Sydney E. Ahlstrom

Puritanism has seldom aroused dispassionate evaluations. In its flowering time it made either enemies or adherents, winning the harshest of judgments from the former, inspiring unbounded self-assurance in the latter. So prevalent was the derogatory use of the term in the early seventeenth century that to some historians the very word "Puritan" is only "an 'x' in the algebra of abuse."[2] Yet to Governor John Winthrop in 1630, the little company of exiles aboard the *Arbella* was embarked on a venture with eternal and divine significance: "Wee must Consider that wee shall be as a Citty vpon a Hill, the eies of all people are vppon vs."[3]

In subsequent years the range of opinion has not materially narrowed. Randolph Bourne, during the First World War, thought Puritanism to be the "real enemy" of American self-fulfillment; and a decade later Van Wyck Brooks made it the fountainhead of all that was mean and narrow in American culture. Yet during these same years Howard A. Bridgman would exhaust the language in extolling the Puritan heritage: "Only . . . in the perfect life that flowered . . . within the narrow limits of Palestine . . . do we find a true historic parallel to the type of power represented by the New England dynamic. For this reason New England is also a holy land." Henry Hallam Saunderson could see Puritan principles as the foundation of American ideals.[4]

Now at mid-century with the air anything but cleared, we are dealing with the relation of this wildly evaluated religious movement to the American democratic spirit. So large is the controversial literature on *this* topic, moreover, that responsible discussion can be opened only after a preliminary consideration of the long debate.

THE INTERPRETATION OF PURITANISM AND DEMOCRACY: FROM WISE TO MILLER

The first point to establish is that we are asking a modern question and not one that any Puritan would have regarded as proper to his apologetic. Professor Morgan has indicated with great precision how Governor Winthrop did in fact widen the franchise in the Bay Colony to a degree unequaled in England and that the political power of the clergy was more limited in the Bay Colony than anywhere in the Western world. That Thomas Hooker and Roger Williams, each in his way, held even more "advanced" views on such matters has also been carefully documented.[5] But no Puritan of the early Holy Commonwealths would have sought to legitimate his enterprise on these grounds. He lived in the fear of God and he would have defended his enterprise by showing that he built his city in strict accordance with God's revealed will.

The earliest significant polemicist to justify the Congregational Way of New England in terms of natural law and right reason was John Wise, an outspoken critic of efforts to impose a connectional or presbyterial church order on Connecticut and Massachusetts. His two controversial pamphlets published in 1710 and 1717 exhibited a frank reliance on the arguments of Pufendorf rather than great Puritan fathers. He was thus an *avant-garde* eccentric working at cross-purposes with the great historical enterprises of Cotton Mather; and quite appropriately he did not receive his due until the 1770's when anti-British patriots put his works back in print. His modern biographer appropriately lauds him as an "early democrat"; we say "appropriately" because John Wise is one of the few among his contemporary ministerial brethren who might have welcomed the title.[6]

The great turning point in Puritan interpretation of the political scene came during the "Revolutionary epoch," which in American history began soon after the expulsion of the French from North America (1759–1763) and extended through the debates and turmoil of the Federalist period (1789–1800). With the White House occupied by the epoch's most eminent Enlightened ideologist, Thomas Jefferson, the time for asking the central question of the present essay had been fully accomplished. The Congregational clergy of New England had, almost to a man, taken their stand for the patriot cause. They had, in fact, given full clerical authority to the refashioned Puritan image that statesmen and political leaders such as John and Samuel Adams had used with such telling effect. The most persuasive pioneer of this "New Whig" revisionism was the liberal minister of Boston's West Church, Jonathan Mayhew (1720–1766). Since Mayhew's career was for all practical purposes lived out before the Stamp Act crisis of 1765, he also serves as an excellent example of the degree to which anti-Anglican (or anti-prelatical) polemics could pave the way for turning old Puritan antipathies for English royal government to the purposes of American self-determination. As these latencies were further exploited during the quarter century after Mayhew's death, it became the almost unanimously accepted practice to praise the early Puritan founders as Whigs, as champions of representative government against royal usurpation, as heroes of political liberty, and even as pioneers of religious freedom.[7]

In this tradition, moreover, proto-Unitarians were, if anything, outdone by orthodox sons of the Puritans. In Lyman Beecher's mind, for example, the Mosaic "republic" of Old Israel, the Holy Commonwealths of early New

England, and the young democratic republic which claimed his fervent loyalty were informed by a common political spirit. He virtually formulated a new argument for the divine origins of Biblical religion by showing the similarity of Mosaic government to the self-evident excellencies of American democracy.[8] During the antebellum heyday of Protestant America, in other words, not only had it become proper to ask *if* there were a positive relationship obtaining between Puritanism and democracy it had become the almost unquestioned assumption of Americans that the relationship was close, obvious, and primary.

To thinkers in this evangelical tradition the special ideological contribution of Enlightened thought was often ignored; in fact, the chief author of the Declaration of Independence was often denounced or remembered as an "infidel." With even larger distorting consequences, America's indebtedness to the legal tradition and institutional development of England was persistently underestimated. There were some American historians of the nineteenth century who transcended these naïve interpretations; but even the greatest of them, George Bancroft, can be charged with an inadequate understanding of Puritanism's essential genius and an exaggeration of its political and libertarian legacy. The same can be said of New England's most exacting and detailed historian, John Gorham Palfrey.[9]

The later nineteenth century, however, brought a drastic revision of the way in which thoughtful Americans understood the several major components of their heritage. One crucial aspect of this change was the theological transformation of the Congregational Church, which was inevitably a special custodian of the Puritan memory. In one of its last great corporate attestations of faith, the "Burial Hill Declaration" of 1865, this denomination did assert its theological affinity with the Puritans.[10] But in the next half century, Congregationalists yielded themselves

almost unanimously to liberal theology and therewith
lost their chief inner line of communication with the
fathers of their tradition.[11] The Puritans (and Jonathan
Edwards with them) usually became the objects of anti-
quarian research, genealogical veneration, uncritical admiration, or hostile reproach. Despite the monumental
historical labors of Henry Martyn Dexter, Franklin Bow-
ditch Dexter, Williston Walker, and George Park Fisher,
the possibilities for understanding the Puritans became
dimmer year by year.

Accompanying and no doubt stimulating this liberaliz-
ing process was the rise of evolutionary, developmental,
and "historicistic" interpretations of human—and American—institutions; interpretations, moreover, that were
usually positivistic in spirit and powerfully informed by
Social Darwinian notions of progress. Riding the crest of
this tendency was the "germ theory" of institutional development that led to a great surge of brilliant historical
activity on the origins and development of legal and
political institutions. Historians under this inspiration
provided still another explanation for American democratic institutions; Anglo-Saxon and German-Saxon origins
were emphasized.[12] It almost became possible in this
ethos to celebrate the victory of Hermann the Great
(Arminius) over the Roman legions of Varus in the
Teutoburger Wald (A.D. 9) as a great saving event for
democracy (much like the battle of Marathon). The contributions of our experience as British colonies were also
more positively appraised.[13] The constructive value of all
this research was very great and its corrective impact on
the Whig interpretation of Puritanism was salutary. At
the same time, nevertheless, these trends served to hinder
serious consideration of the dynamic interrelationships
between Puritanism and democracy that have in fact obtained in the United States.

Progressivism, the social gospel, religious liberalism,
the First World War, and "normalcy" did not provide a

suitable climate for significant revisions of America's self-understanding, especially as it related to the Puritans. Even the fulsome affirmations of Woodbridge and Sauderson (already referred to or quoted) were little more than thoughtless reiterations of the legends of national romanticism. What did change the picture was the intellectual, spiritual, and theological revolution that characterized the years between the great crash of 1929 and the outbreak of the Second World War. Yet these dates are somewhat arbitrary. As always, there were precursors; and as something like a self-conscious movement of reassessment came into existence, a long supportive tradition was also clarified.

The term "neoorthodoxy" suggests one aspect of this new intellectual impulse; but it soon became clear that the transition had secular as well as religious or theological implications.[14] Reinhold Niebuhr's *Moral Man and Immoral Society* in 1932 served, indeed, to keynote both the secular and the theological aspects of the turning point. That year was also memorable for Joseph Haroutunian's eloquent and forceful reevaluation of Jonathan Edwards and his successors. In 1936, H. Richard Niebuhr's *Kingdom of God in America* extended this reassessment to the Reformation, the Puritans, and the nineteenth-century evangelicals. Most important of all for our special problem, Perry Miller began his extraordinary career as a reinterpreter of Puritanism with an incisive analysis of "Thomas Hooker and the Democracy of Connecticut" (1931), to be followed in 1935 by his finest essay, "The Marrow of Puritan Divinity," and then one after another a steady stream of trenchant essays and massive treatises on *Orthodoxy in Massachusetts* (1933), *The New England Mind* (1939, 1953), and *Jonathan Edwards* (1949).[15]

It was neither strange nor accidental that Miller's overhauling of the prevailing Puritan image should have begun when it did. In 1955, on being honored by the Congregational Historical Society, Professor Miller made

one of his rare public confessions as to why he had begun
these laborious researches. It was due, he said, to

a dissatisfaction which, even as a very callow student, I felt
with nineteenth-century treatments of the seventeenth century.
I could see even then, and see even more clearly now, that
the scholarship was indeed excellent and thorough. This is a
fitting occasion to express my immense admiration for, as well
as my incalculable debt to, such mighty scholars as John
Gorham Palfrey, Henry Martyn Dexter, Williston Walker,
George Fisher, Frank Hugh Foster. If I have been able to
contribute anything over and above what these learned men
formulated, it is only because I came of age after the First
World War, in what has by now come to be generally termed
an Age of Anxiety. The optimism of the well-bred mind in the
nineteenth century was so pervasive, irresistible, you might
even say unconscious, that men of this stamp were hopelessly
cut off from the innermost mood of the Covenant Theology.
In America, concepts of individualism, free enterprise, self-
reliance, the right to make money, of indefinite and inexhausti-
ble prosperity, had become so identified with the eternal law
of Almighty God that by no stretch of the historical imagina-
ion could these well-intentioned researchers share in the dread
that lay at the heart of the Puritan experiment. They felt, and
rightly, that even though emancipated from Calvinism they
could sympathetically understand the mentality of individual
Calvinists; what they could not comprehend, for they had no
clue for comprehending, was that the individual drama in a
Puritan community was enacted amid an enveloping concern
about social destiny. I think I may say that such opposition as
my books have encountered—or rather, such deficiency of full
appreciation even on the part of those wanting to be friendly
—seems to me attributable in great part to the fact that many
of my readers, especially those somewhat older than I am,
have remained in the clutch of that stubborn, persistent, in-
domitable, optimism that inspired the gigantic growth and
prosperity of this country.[16]

Miller, on the other hand, had begun this very paper with
the suggestion that the materialistic culture of the United
States might exhaust itself and that the nation's power
and world prestige might not be so appropriately likened
to the Roman Empire as to the Parthian!

The purpose of this extensive quotation is not to argue that a pessimistic view of the American destiny was necessary to a right understanding of either Puritanism or democracy, but simply to indicate that the renaissance of Puritan scholarship during the last quarter century is meaningfully related to the country's overall intellectual experience. It also may serve as a small tribute to the achievement of Perry Miller, whose life came to an untimely end on December 9, 1963. These autobiographical lines from one of his least known essays seem especially valuable now. Finally, we may note that the passage does come to rest precisely on the problem we are addressing —with an insistence that in Puritan eyes the *commonwealth* was God's means for effecting his will on earth. With this assertion setting the tone for what follows, it is now well to grapple more directly with the issue.

FORMS OF INTERPRETATION

In the literature on the contribution of the Puritans to American democracy there have been four rather persistent traditions of interpretation. (1) The earliest of these has always been the stock in trade of the anti-Puritans: it holds that Puritans were insufferable, self-righteous precisionists with narrow minds and blue noses, authoritarian, clericalist, intolerant, and antidemocratic. Their contribution is inconsequential; Puritan "declension" is simply another term for the rise of the democratic spirit. John Adams' great-grandson Brooks Adams stated the matter plainly—the story of Puritanism's loosening hold is the story of *The Emancipation of Massachusetts*.[17] (2) A somewhat later and more refined version of this same interpretation is that which relents to the extent of singling out certain exceptional—and allegedly atypical— Puritans and depicting these as great democratic pioneers whose enlightened labors stand in sharp contrast to a dark theocratic background. The men most often depicted in this light are Roger Williams, Thomas Hooker, William

Penn, and the aforementioned John Wise. Most interpreters in this category make vast assumptions about the
actual historical influence of their particular hero; and
some of them base their whole case on a gross distortion
of the Puritan movement as a whole.[18] (3) The Whig
interpretation in either its Enlightened or Romantic modes
is another possibility, and the one that has come closest
to becoming part of American folklore.[19] My convictions
as to its inadequacy as a theory underlie the entire first
section of this essay. (4) Finally there is a cluster of
interpretations that seek in the first place to understand
Puritanism sympathetically and in its own terms and then
consider the ways in which that intense movement of
religious awakening modified the spirit and texture of
democratic life in the United States. The most germinal
thinking of this last mentioned type has been done by
Max Weber and Ernst Troeltsch, with special concern for
changing economic attitudes. The title chosen for this
essay is in part an acknowledgment of my own indebtedness to the sociological and historical work that these men
and their successors have done.[20]

In making clear how such an analysis of Puritan belief
and piety fits into a full historical account of American
democracy, one may distinguish three major aspects of
the democratic tradition, each of which has been profit-
ably studied with regard to its origins, its development,
and the forces (economic or otherwise) that have conditioned it.

1. The *institutions* of democracy, that is, the executive
offices, legislatures, courts, and procedures by means of
which a democratic government receives its authority
and performs its assigned functions.

2. The *ideals and theories* of democracy, that is, the
principles that inform, animate and, to a degree, shape
the structures of government and define their relations to
the people; and also the theories and philosophies of man,
society, and government by which these principles are ex-

plained, defended, and related to the larger human and historical context.

3. The *sense of civic responsibility* which animates the citizenry and magistracy, that is, the moral attitudes of the people toward governmental functions, governors and judges, law and order, civic duties and rights.

These are by no means exhaustive categories; yet each of them is obviously important. With regard to the United States, moreover, the impact of Puritanism has often been discussed in all three respects, though the first two, and especially the second, have received most attention. It is my belief that these efforts to emphasize Puritan contributions to the institutions or theory of democracy have never seemed convincing unless stated in exceedingly modest terms. Special pleading of any sort has almost invariably tended to distort or veil the Puritan's chief intention, which was not to work reforms in the legal and governmental systems of England.[21] I will concentrate, therefore, on the third theme.

PURITANISM AND CIVIC RESPONSIBILITY

The first desire of the chief leaders, greatest exemplars, and most characteristic spokesmen of New England's early Holy Commonwealths was for true churches wherein God's Word would be rightly preached and wherein his ordinances would be rightly administered to those for whom God intended them. They emigrated from England and founded governments that would foster and protect such churches. *We do well, therefore, to search out the consequences for American democracy of this primary Puritan concern;* and this leads us not so much to new political theories or new institutions (though life on the New World frontier would lead to innovations in both areas) as to a new kind of civic ethos or moral climate. It is upon the *spirit* of American democracy that Puritanism worked its most direct and powerful effects; and if we look to the center of the Puritan faith, we may perceive the springs of its peculiar power to mold personal values, to gird the citizen or magistrate for his work, to arouse and maintain his sense of civic duty, to intensify his determination to live responsibly before and under the law, and to make him aware that neither individual men, or groups of men, or even nations were above the law or were laws unto themselves. These were the areas where Puritanism made its profoundest contributions both in England and in America. In these areas, moreover, Puritan nurture continued to have powerful shaping effect on succeeding generations even after the original standards were relaxed.

The special moral or civic qualities of American democracy have been commented upon by many keen observers, though few have sought a historical explanation of what they saw. Consider first the commentary of Francis Grund (1798–1863), who emigrated from Austria to the United States in 1827. He published a very important book on *The Americans in Their Moral, Social, and Political Relations* in 1837, and his *Aristocracy in America* two years later. In the latter he reflects on one occasion that the "bright points" of the New Englander's character are best seen "in his relation to the community as a citizen."

Few people have so great respect for the law, and are so well able to govern themselves. . . . Though their State politics have generally been inclined towards Whig, and even Toryism, they are nevertheless the most thorough Radicals in principle, and, perhaps, the only people capable of enjoying so large a portion of liberty without abusing it. In addition to this they are sober, industrious, and, with the exception of a few straggling pedlars . . . just and honourable in their dealings.

Grund concludes this passage with the observation that "nature has done everything to make them calm, sober republicans."[22] But one wonders if Puritans would not provide a more satisfactory explanation than "nature."

In his other book Grund widened the scope of his generalizations:

I consider the domestic virtue of the Americans as the principal source of all their other qualities. It acts as a promoter of industry, as a stimulus to enterprise, and as the most powerful restrainer of public vice. . . . No government could be established on the same principle as that of the United States, with a different code of morals. The American Constitution is remarkable for its simplicity; but it can only suffice a people habitually correct in their actions, and would be utterly inadequate to the wants of a different nation. Change the domestic habits of the Americans, their religious devotion, and their high respect for morality, and it will not be necessary to change a single letter of the Constitution in order to vary the whole form of their government.[23]

The most famous of all the foreign interpreters of American democracy was Alexis de Tocqueville, who traveled in the United States in 1831–1832. He too points to the importance of a certain kind of public virtue:

In the United States everyone is personally interested in enforcing the obedience of the whole community to the law. . . . However irksome an enactment may be, the citizen of the United States complies with it, not only because it is the work of the majority, but because it is his own, and he regards it as a contract to which he is himself a party.
In the United States, then, that numerous and turbulent multitude does not exist who, regarding the law as their natural enemy, look upon it with fear and distrust. It is impossible, on the contrary, not to perceive that all classes display the utmost reliance upon the legislation of their country and are attached to it by a kind of parental affection.[24]

Some might feel that Tocqueville was too adulatory; yet it is interesting that Lord Bryce, who published his great study of the United States a half century later, still felt the prevalence of civic concern to be a major strength of American democracy:

Feeling the law to be its own work, the people is disposed to obey the law. In a preceding chapter I have examined occasional instances of the disregard of the law. . . . Such instances [however] scarcely affect the credit which the Americans are specially eager to claim of being a law-abiding community.

There is in the United States a sort of kindliness, a sense of human fellowship, a recognition of the duty of mutual help owed by man to man, stronger than anywhere in the Old World, and certainly stronger than in the upper or middle classes of England, France, or Germany. The natural impulse of every citizen in America is to respect every other citizen, and to feel that citizenship constitutes a certain ground of respect.[25]

During World War II another English interpreter wrote a further variation on this theme. Speaking of the United States during the nineteenth century, Denis Brogan observed that "no government that had any claim to be a government at all has had less direct power over the people it ruled." Yet, he goes on to say:

If there was a good deal of lawlessness, there was real respect for law. There was a general acceptance of the authority of the State and the Union. There was no equivalent of Spanish-American revolutions, no encouragement given to mere *pronunciamentos*, though a man like Andrew Jackson in a Spanish environment would have had all the talents and temperament and temptations of a dictator. But Jackson and his followers and enemies gave to the Constitution of the United States the reverence due to 'the supreme law of the land.' . . . No society could have grown so fast if the minimum basis of law had not been provided by the free choice of the people, the only effective authority.[26]

The point made over and over again by these and many other observers of democracy in the United States is that Americans are, by and large, a law-abiding people with a strong sense of civic responsibility. And this despite a history of tumultuous expansion and change that would seem to have given every opportunity to barbarism, anarchy, and chaos. Not one of these critics, moreover, has been blind to serious American shortcomings; nor do I, in quoting their judgments, wish to appear unrealistic or self-congratulatory. We simply are face to face with a remarkable and somewhat paradoxical heritage. And I would stress the impossibility of understanding either the remarkableness or the paradoxicality of the American civic character aside from the country's essentially Puritan origins and the continuous process—secular and churchly —by which Puritan values and insistences have not only been handed down from generation to generation but have actually been built into the country's social habits and conventions. In this perspective, one sees the utter propriety of President John F. Kennedy's explicitly identifying himself as a Roman Catholic and third-generation Irish-American with the Puritan spirit and legacy.[27]

THE DIVINE SOVEREIGNTY

The proper starting place in the quest for an understanding of this dynamic fact in American history is the cardinal doctrine of the Judeo-Christian tradition: divine sovereignty. In no tradition did this tenet become more central an affirmation than in the Reformed movement that came to recognize John Calvin as its greatest spokesman. In the family of "Reformed" churches, furthermore, probably none was so determined to work out the social ethics implicit in such views as those Puritans who were the architects and leading spirits of the several colonial governments in British North America. And of these none were so articulate, so determined, and so influential on latter-day American history as the founders of New England's Holy Commonwealths. If we can reach to *their* deepest convictions, we can touch a dominant theme in our history.

The Puritan's most consequential conviction can be stated as follows: he had a rigorous, awe-filled concern for God's almighty will as that was revealed in Scripture. This legalism, this conviction that the Bible, through command, counsel, and historical example, provided precise divine guidance for church, state, and personal life set Puritans apart and won them their reputation for "precisionism." This concern for the law drove Puritans to repudiate centuries of "human tradition" in ordering the government and worship of the Christian church.[28] It shaped their understanding of personal discipline and of the Christian's proper relationship to all the structures of society: the family, the marketplace, the school, and the state. Ancient Israel, moreover, became for them a veritable model in both civil and ecclesiastical matters, and in the interrelation of the two.[29] Indeed John Cotton knit together these conceptions of ecclesiastical and civil government very early in his New England ministry (1636): "It is better that the commonwealth be fashioned to the setting forth of Gods house, which is his church: than to accomodate the church frame to the civil state. Democracy, I do not conceyve that ever God did ordeyne as a fitt government eyther for church or commonwealth. If the people be governors, who shall be governed?"[30] Christians were regarded as being under the law even when they were choosing ministers to be over them.

It was the same in civil affairs. At the very outset of Connecticut's political history such a conception also lay behind the second head of Thomas Hooker's famous sermon to the colony's lawmakers: "The privilege of election, which belongs to the people, . . . must not be exercized according to their humours, but according to the blessed will and law of God."[31] Governor John Winthrop of the Massachusetts Bay Colony had a somewhat stronger view of "magistratical authority" than did Hooker, but on fundamentals the two men agreed that governors and people were under God's rule:

There is a two fold liberty [said Winthrop to the General Court in 1645] natural . . . and civil or federal. The first is common to man with beasts and other creatures. . . . The other kind of liberty . . . may also be termed moral, in reference to the covenant between God and man, in the moral law, and the politic covenants and constitutions, amongst men themselves. . . . This liberty is maintained and exercised in a way of subjection to authority; it is of the same kind of liberty

wherewith Christ hath made us free. . . . Such is the liberty of
the church under the authority of Christ, her king and husband. . . . Even so, brethren, it will be between you and your
magistrates . . . if you will be satisfied to enjoy such civil and
lawful liberties, such as Christ allows you, then will you
quietly and cheerfully submit unto that authority which is set
over you. . . .[32]

These various passages, taken together, also serve to emphasize the Puritan's nearly total disinclination for considering their religious task in individualistic terms. It
was a "city" they were building; like Israel of old, they
were involved in a corporate venture. Theirs was a commonwealth with a divine mission.

THE DIVINE CALLING

Additional impetus to an aroused civic concern came
from the new conception of the *calling* unleashed by the
Reformation generally and stressed with special intensity
by the Puritans.[33] The relation of this new ethical emphasis on the spirit and growth of capitalism was a particular
scholarly concern of Max Weber,[34] but the vast literature
that has grown up in response to his provocative essays
gives rise to two considerations in the present context.

First and most obviously, the Puritan doctrine of vocation was by no means restricted to the world's *economic*
structures, for every Christian also had a vocation in the
political order as a citizen or magistrate. Quite aside from
the impact of economic life on the political realm, therefore, the Puritan ethic, as my quotations have suggested,
also dealt with political duty directly. On this subject
Increase Mather summed up seventy years of American
Puritan preaching in his Election Sermon of 1702. Speaking on "The Excellency of a Publick Spirit," he pointed to
"the great Evil which is in being a private self-seeking
Spirit." "The Lord Jesus Christ [he declared] will take
notice of them before all the world at the last day, who
have with a sincere heart sought the Welfare of his
people."[35]

Nor was it only through such direct exhortation that a solemn view of civic duty was implanted; as in the economic realm so in the political, the importance of man's vocation was also strengthened by the overall system of doctrine and piety. My second point, in fact, emphasizes these *indirect* effects. Max Weber, to be sure, in his discussion of capitalism dealt with these effects very profoundly. Yet his writings on the need to understand the significance for secular pursuits of a *total* religious outlook were at best incomplete.[36] Nearly all his critics, and even some of his champions, have given a very cramped and mechanistic interpretation to his ideas. We need further emphasis, therefore, on the way in which the Reformed and Puritan outlook *as a whole* provided a kind of inner, subjective support to faithful and serious performance of these worldly callings—whether they be in the family, the marketplace, or in the state. Such internal relationships are hardly able to be verified quantitatively; but if they are carefully explored and sensitively interpreted, they do much to illumine our historical understanding of the spirit and working of American democracy.

GOD'S HAMMER

Of all the factors that contribute to the moral impact of Puritanism, perhaps none has such vast civic implications as the way in which the manifold workings of the law—divine, natural, and civil—were applied to the Puritan's central affirmations as to God's means for ordering a sinful world and for redeeming his elect. The law was a judge, God's hammer, by which man's pride was brought low. "Legal terrors," contrition, repentance, and the soul's humiliation were the steps to regeneration. And in the eyes of most Puritans it was by preparing the soul in the light of God's conditional promises that a person was made ready for saving experience.

For one who had experienced the saving work of the Holy Spirit the law continued to be a guide to holiness under the "covenant of evangelical obedience." The law was thus not only a judge but a teacher, and for both saint and sinner. Christian freedom was freedom under the law as Winthrop so clearly stated; and nowhere would "antinomianism" be viewed with such violent antipathy as in the Bible Commonwealths.[37]

The most revealing encounter of "nomianism" and "antinomianism" in early New England was precipitated by a remarkable disciple of John Cotton in the Boston church. Anne Hutchinson's charges that most of the Bay Colony's ministers were preaching a "Covenant of Works" may have reflected an overly excited piety; but there is no denying that her attack on law-centered (hence moralistic) doctrines of preparation and sanctification struck to the heart of the prevailing theology. She was, therefore, denounced by a specially convened synod, excommunicated by her congregation, and exiled by the civil authorities. She cast her lot with the Holy Spirit rather than the law; and she was clearly a subversive.[38]

According to the view that thereafter came to be accepted as correct, a God-fearing "visible saint" was in the deepest, most thoroughgoing sense of the term a law-abiding person, even though he must also experience an internal work of grace. As the years went by, however, the accent shifted steadily away from the experience of regeneration and toward law-abidingness. "Legal terrors" became a memory—if that, with the Great Awakening bringing only a temporary reassertion of experientialism. Piety yielded to moralism, and the Puritan gradually became a Yankee, with Benjamin Franklin, the most brilliant examplar of that new breed, revealing both its limitations and its excellences.[39]

From the traditional Puritan point of view, this entire process was "declension" and a vast homiletical literature of lamentation arose. One aspect of the trend, nevertheless, could be neither lamented nor denied: in the political order men continued to be called to obedience and civic responsibility. And as the accent on law-abidingness grew, so did the optimistic conviction that even unregenerate human nature could aspire to moral perfection. This movement culminates in both the vision and the sense of civic duty exhibited in the Revolutionary epoch by many of the new nation's Founding Fathers.

THE CONTINUING INFLUENCE OF PURITANISM

It is not at all mysterious that men should move in this direction. Neither is it strange, considering the moral intensity and traditionary force of the whole Puritan ethos, that men should continue to propagate and live by the secularized principles with the same vigor and austerity. Puritanism thus can almost be said to have offered itself as a sacrifice to responsible citizenship. It declined with surprising swiftness, but was enormously influential almost because it was so readily secularized. Its "secularizability," in fact, is an important clue to the movement's long-term civic significance. Knowing this, we can share the poignant historical observation of George W. Pierson: "Just as with the philosophy of the Greeks, or the laws laid down by the Romans, the moral attitudes of New England culture persist though the people who gave them birth have long since passed away."[40]

The disappearance of classic Puritanism did not end its influence however. The Great Awakening of the eighteenth century kept alive some dimensions of the Puritan impulse. The "Revolutionary generation" renovated and enlivened the old sense of the country's mission in a way that was by no means utterly secular (see the several devices on our national seal on any dollar bill). And the great evangelical revivals beginning after 1790 made the entire nineteenth century a time of evangelical resurgence in which Puritan and Enlightened notions of the national purpose were blended.[41] Throughout this process, moreover, the idea of civic responsibility as a Christian virtue was a corollary of the American's confidence in his country's political *and* religious destiny and his refusal as a practical matter to separate church and state. On this subject, too, Francis Grund offered a valuable observation:

It is with the solemnities of religion that the Declaration of Independence is yet annually read to the people from the pulpit or that Americans celebrate the anniversaries of the most important events in their history. . . . The Americans look upon religion as a promoter of civil and political liberty; and have, therefore, transferred to it a large portion of the affection which they cherish for the institutions of their country. In other countries, where religion has become the instrument of oppression, it has been the policy of the liberal party to diminish its influence; but in America its promotion is essential to the constitution.[42]

Americans are not now faultless paragons of dutiful citizenship and responsible governance. Sober analysts, indeed, are speaking of a moral crisis. Violence and irresponsibility in our public life have shocked the world and scarred a generation of Americans. Yet the tradition as a whole has also been a beacon—even a marvel—to the world; and there is in it profound occasion for gratitude. A portion of this gratitude, moreover, is due to the Puritan's total view of man's state under God's rule, to his explicit concern for law, duty, public spirit, and the commonweal, and to the fact that he framed his counsels in such a way that their efficacy continued long after the movement's flourishing time. In the grounds for and the fruits of that concern lies the chief political legacy of Puritanism.

Chapter 6
John Locke: Heir of
Puritan Political Theorists
By Winthrop S. Hudson

John Locke was made to order for those who sought
to defend the rights of the American colonists in the years
preceding the American Revolution. On the one hand,
his political thought was thoroughly acceptable in America because it was a restatement of familiar principles—
principles forged by the heirs of John Calvin during the
English Civil Wars and long the common property of most
of colonial America. On the other hand, as the chief
apologist of the Glorious Revolution of 1688 which
brought William and Mary to the English and Scottish
thrones, Locke was eminently respectable. The great
utility of being able to quote Locke rather than the earlier
Puritan political theorists was noted by James Otis. To
have cited the Puritan writers, Otis observed, would have
given an excuse for the opponents of the colonial cause to
raise the cry of rebellion.[1] While the tactic of quoting
Locke had obvious propagandist value, few contemporaries either in Britain or America were misled as to the
source of Locke's ideas. Edmund Burke and John Adams
were both aware of the pit from whence the political
principles of Locke had been dug,[2] and the cartoons of
the time made it evident that the general populace was
equally clear in its understanding that Locke and Sidney
and Calvin were representatives of a single tradition.[3]

If the Revolutionary generation was not misled by the
propagandist tactic of appealing to Locke instead of ap-

pealing to the Puritan controversialists whose sentiments
he reiterated, subsequent generations have been misled.
Most modern scholars have tended to regard Burke and
Otis and Adams as either ill-informed or not quite bright
in attributing Locke's ideas to the sons of Geneva, and
they have pictured Locke's political thought as something
new, modern, different, "secular." Having posited this
discontinuity, they have then been puzzled by what they
could only regard as the strange alliance of "rationalists"
and "pietists" in the colonists' struggle for "liberty both
civil and ecclesiastical."

This misunderstanding of Locke was made possible in
part by the fact that Locke also had been careful not to
call attention to the source from which he derived his
political principles. He too had no desire to raise the cry
of sedition by appealing to the writings of the Puritan
revolutionists of the 1640's. Whenever he could he cited
"the judicious Hooker," in spite of the fact that he dis-
sented from Hooker at numerous decisive points.[4] Unfortunately this gave a false lead to pedantic scholars who
are fond of counting citations as an index of influence.
Having been led to Richard Hooker by this false scent and
believing that the key to Locke's thought was his concept
of natural law, many scholars then scurried around seeking to find evidence of a continuing natural law tradition
among some of the more emancipated minds of the century that intervened between Hooker's great work and the
publication of Locke's treatises. The writings of Chilling-
worth, Cudworth, Culverwel, Stillingfleet, and Whichcote
were culled with fine-tooth combs to find further clues
to Locke's dependence upon his predecessors, but the
Puritan tracts and sermons were generally ignored as belonging to another genre in spite of the fact that an appeal
to natural law was one of the most characteristic features
of their writings.

Further confusion was introduced by a misunderstanding and misinterpretation of Locke's terminology. When-

ever Locke used the word "civil"—as in "civil government" and "civil order"—the word "civil" was generally interpreted to mean "secular." And Locke's references to "natural law" and "natural rights" were interpreted as an appeal to "secular" authority. No one schooled in Puritan political theory would have read this meaning into these terms. Equally confusing was Locke's use of the word "religion" as an antonym of "civil." "Civil" embraced the ordinary things of this life, the outward affairs of life, things pertaining to temporal peace and order. "Religion," as Locke used the word, had to do with inward matters, matters relating to the soul of man, to one's salvation, to the life to come, to eternal peace. But for Locke, God was not absent in the civil order. It also was under the rule of God and was to be ordered according to his will. Locke's difficulty stemmed largely from the poverty of the English language at this point. Other writers had sought to avoid this ambiguity by using "soul causes" and "spiritual" as antonyms of "civil," but these terms were frequently awkward and presented other problems of definition.

It is true, of course, that theologically and philosophically Locke was the heir of Puritan rationalism. Those who viewed Locke from the vantage-point of knowing the future course that this tradition was to take may have had some excuse for seeing him as the forerunner of the modern secularist liberal. But this is not an adequate excuse, for Locke must be understood in terms of his own thought and not in terms of what the rationalists of a much later generation were to make of it. Nor is it likely that Locke would have escaped such misinterpretation had he belonged to the more pietistically inclined wing of Puritanism, for even such an unreconstructed pietist as Roger Williams was cut to the pattern of a nineteenth-century liberal by Vernon L. Parrington, James Ernst, and other modern interpreters. Nor did A. S. P. Woodhouse, who made such a brilliant analysis of the Puritan contribution to liberty, wholly avoid the temptation to equate references to the "civil order" and "natural law" with secularism.[5] But neither John Milton's contemporaries nor those of Locke would have made this mistake. And certainly the "pietists" of the Revolutionary generation in America, as the heirs of the older Puritan tradition, would not have read Locke in this way.

Who was John Locke? Locke's father was an ardent Puritan, a captain of the horse in the parliamentary army. Locke's early patron, who arranged for him to attend the Westminster School in London, was an equally ardent Puritan, a colonel of the parliamentary forces, and after 1645 a member of the Long Parliament. From 1646 to 1652 Locke was at Westminster within a stone's throw of the momentous events that culminated in the execution of the king and of the debates that followed over the proper form of government to be adopted. When Locke secured a studentship at Christ Church, Oxford in 1652, John Owen, the noted Independent divine and strong advocate of broad religious toleration, was dean of Christ Church and vice-chancellor of the university (Oliver Cromwell filled the largely honorary post of chancellor). Locke's tutor at Oxford was Thomas Cole, another Independent divine, who was later to establish the dissenting academy at which Samuel Wesley received his education and still later was to succeed Philip Nye as minister of an Independent congregation in London. The professor of history at Oxford, whose lectures Locke was compelled to attend, was that "fiery" Independent Louis du Moulin.[6] Du Moulin was the son of Pierre du Moulin, the teacher of Grotius, and he was addicted to notions of popular sovereignty, fundamental law, natural rights, liberty of conscience, government based upon contract and popular consent, simplification of ceremonies, and churches as voluntary associations. None of this, of course, was new or novel. It had become the common stock-in-trade of the Independents as a whole.

By the time of the Restoration of the Stuarts in 1660, Locke had rejected the party affiliation of his father. He had become an ardent Royalist and an extreme authoritarian. With Thomas Hobbes he believed that any government was better than no government, and that only a strong government could put an end to the conflict and strife that had prevailed. In 1661 he wrote a vigorous answer to *The Great Question concerning Things Indifferent* (1660), a tract by Edward Bagshaw, Jr.[7] To this plea for toleration, Locke replied that "the magistrate of every nation . . . must necessarily have an absolute and arbitrary power over all the indifferent actions of his people."[8]

By 1665 Locke had begun to have second thoughts. He had become disenchanted with the fruits of the rigorous policy imposed by the new Stuart regime. In November of that year he went on an embassy to Brandenburg as secretary to Walter Vane, brother of Henry Vane the Younger who had been governor of Massachusetts, Cromwell's key parliamentary lieutenant, and an uncompromising republican. At Brandenburg Locke found a broad policy of toleration in operation that included Lutherans, Calvinists, and Roman Catholics. "They quietly permit one another to choose their way to heaven," he wrote, "and I cannot observe any quarrels or animosities amongst them on account of religion." They "entertain different opinions without any secret hatred or rancor."[9] When Locke returned to England he began to jot down his ideas on toleration, putting them together in 1667 in an unpublished essay.[10] Here one finds the basic ideas and frequently the language of his famous *Letter concerning Toleration*, written in 1685 and published in 1689.

By the time he had written the *Essay concerning Toleration*, Locke had become an employee and adviser of Anthony Ashley Cooper, who was to become the first Earl of Shaftesbury in 1672. Cooper also had been one of Cromwell's close collaborators and like Vane had broken with Cromwell when Cromwell seemed determined to retain his autocratic powers. Cooper had made his peace with the Stuarts in 1660 and was made lord chancellor in 1672. When Cooper, now Lord Shaftesbury, fell from power in 1675, Locke retired to France "for his health." During this four-year period in France, Locke was in intimate contact with many French Calvinists. When Shaftesbury was restored to favor and made president of the council, Locke returned to England. In 1683, when his patron once more fell under royal disfavor, Locke again sought refuge on the Continent and remained there until William and Mary came to the throne. This time he spent his exile in the Netherlands, where he found a kindred spirit and close friend in the person of the "Remonstrant" theologian, Philip van Limborch, who represented the liberal Calvinism of Jacobus Arminius.[11]

Where did Locke derive his political ideas? With regard to his general political principles one need not look far. They were being shouted from the housetops during the years he was at Westminster and Oxford, and they had been explicated again and again by the sons of Geneva with whom he was in contact throughout his life. Even a conservative Presbyterian like Samuel Rutherford, in *Lex rex* (1644) (see the preceding chapter in this volume), invoked almost every argument that was later used by Locke, including an appeal to the law of nature, the ultimate sovereignty of the people, the origin of government in a contract between the governor and the governed, and the right of resistance when that contract is broken. The question of religious toleration, however, is more complex and needs more detailed attention.

At least three principles were involved in the development of Puritan thought concerning toleration. For convenience we may call them the principle of fallibility, the principle of segregation, and the principle of consent.

The principle of fallibility had its roots in the Protestant Reformation. A basic postulate of the Reformation was the insistence that all men are fallible and that even General Councils have erred and may err. This was a principle, when taken seriously, that tended to undercut any program of enforced religious conformity, for it compelled an acknowledgment that any dominant group might be wrong and that even a lone dissenter might be right.

People seldom perceive at once the full implications of the principles they profess. In actual fact, the disturbing implications of the principle of fallibility were pushed into the background by most Protestants until the non-Separatist wing of the English Independents made use of the principle of fallibility during the two decades prior to 1640 to justify their separate worship while at the same time they affirmed themselves to be loyal sons of the Church of England. To this end they formulated a four-point argument. First, they pointed to the possibility of further truth being made known from the written Word of God. Second, they asserted that further truth had been made known to them and that as faithful and obedient Christians they were under obligation to make their practice conform to the measure of light they had received, reserving always a liberty "to alter and retract (though not lightly) whatever should be discovered to be taken up out of a misunderstanding of the rule." Third, they remembered their frailty in their former way of conformity and consequently were unwilling to judge harshly and uncharitably those of their former brethren who did not see all things as clearly as did they. For this reason they would not deny them the name of Christian nor renounce them as utterly corrupt and without any measure of grace. Fourth, they hoped for equal charitableness and indulgence from those—whether Episcopalians or Presbyterians—from whom they were forced to dissent.[12] Initially these Independents thought of toleration in no larger terms than an "accommodation" that would permit them liberty of conscience, but they were appealing to a principle that was to make it exceedingly difficult for them to deny to others the same freedom that they claimed for themselves.

By the middle 1640's an increasing number of this group had been forced to acknowledge that if a lone dissenter might be right, God's Spirit must be free to blow where it listeth. Every man must be free to speak and to listen, to convince and to be convinced. "How can truth appear but by argumentation?" asked John Cook in explicating what the Independents would have. "Sparks are beaten out by the flints striking together," asserted Jeremiah Burroughes. How can men, he continued, "know that they are right . . . , till they, by discussing, praying, reading, meditating, find that out?" Furthermore, as the author of *The Ancient Bounds, or Liberty of Conscience, Tenderly Stated, Modestly Asserted, and Mildly Vindicated* (1645) insisted, "this liberty of free disquisition is as great a means to keep the truth as to find it."[13]

Of more decisive importance for an understanding of Locke's thought was the principle of segregation that A. S. P. Woodhouse has so carefully analyzed. This principle was also an inheritance from the Reformation and it stood at the very center of Puritan thought. Nowhere was it stated more clearly than in *The Ancient Bounds:*

Christ Jesus, whose is the kingdom, the power, and the glory, both in nature and grace, hath given several maps and schemes of his dominions . . . ; both of his great kingdom, the world, . . . which he hath committed to men to be administered in truth and righteousness in a various form as they please . . . ; and also of his special or peculiar kingdom, the kingdom of grace. . . .

And not only man in society, but every man individually is an epitome, either of one only or of both these dominions. Of one only [the kingdom of the world], so every natural man . . . in whose conscience God hath his throne, ruling him by the light of nature to a civil outward good and end. Of both [the kingdom of the world and the kingdom of grace], so every believer who, besides this natural conscience and rule, hath an enlightened conscience, carrying a more bright and lively stamp of the kingly place and power of the Lord Jesus.[14]

This distinction between the two realms of nature and grace was susceptible of two interpretations.

The dominant view initially was that God's special kingdom took precedence over his general kingdom. While the life of grace was possible only to the elect, the nonelect were to be brought within the context of a national church where they could be disciplined to the glory of God and brought into outward conformity to the standards of the godly.

The second interpretation grew out of dissatisfaction generated by the failure to effect a thoroughgoing reform of the national church. Among those who were distressed by this failure, the conviction developed that, since the life of grace was attainable by the elect alone, its proper expression was not a national church (a mixed multitude) but a voluntary community of visible saints who would be able to bring their church life into conformity with their Christian profession.

A further corollary that was deduced from the fact that the life of grace was beyond the capacity of natural men was an insistence that the life of the larger community could be regulated only in terms of that kingdom wherein God rules men, as the author of *The Ancient Bounds* put it, "by the light of nature to a civil outward good and end." This did not mean that the saints were not concerned with the life of the larger society, nor did it mean that the civil magistrate was not a minister of God in his appointed vocation. It simply meant that the saints lived in two different realms, each with its own distinct God-given end. In the one realm they found their guidelines in God's special revelation in Christ; in the other realm they found their guidelines in God's general revelation in natural reason. In the one realm, where unbelievers were excluded by definition, coercion was unavailing and the saints were limited to the influence they could exert by exhortation and example; in the other realm, whose end was the preservation of the bodies and goods of men, compulsion was appropriate, since the use of force could serve this end.

The third principle was the principle of consent. Since no one can be coerced by anyone but God into being a Christian, the church must be voluntary. This meant, as Richard Mather pointed out, that "churches have no power over such as have not engaged themselves by covenant, and committed power unto them by professing to be subject to all the ordinances of Christ amongst them." *The Saints' Apology* put it more tersely: "Which jurisdiction no man can lawfully be subjected unto but by his own agreement."[15] Ecclesiastical life belonged to the realm of grace and was beyond the reach of the civil magistrate. There could be no compulsion. There could be only a voluntary subjection to the discipline of the church. Even among the Independents there was much hesitation at this point. Many were fearful of limiting the magistrate to obligations imposed by natural reason. This was notably true in New England, but in old England both the logic of their thought and the pressure of events quickly pushed them to the conclusion that found expression in Oliver Cromwell's assertion that "liberty of conscience is a natural right"[16] and in John Milton's declaration that "civil power neither hath right nor can do right by forcing religious things."[17]

This type of thinking is familiar to anyone who has read Locke's *Letter concerning Toleration,* for Locke did no more than restate the argument that had been fashioned by Independent divines. Locke was undoubtedly acquainted with and indebted to the writings of John Goodwin, John Milton, John Owen, Jeremiah Burroughes, and many others, including the author of *The Ancient Bounds.* The parallels with the thought of Roger Williams, however, are so close that it is not an entirely implausible conjecture to suggest that Locke's major contribution may have been to reduce the rambling, lengthy, and incoherent exposition of the New England "firebrand" to orderly, abbreviated, and coherent form. Beyond a differing emphasis and concern, it is impossible to discover a single

significant difference between the argument set forth by
Williams and that later advanced by Locke. They scarcely
differ even in the details of its practical application.

Locke begins by reaffirming the principle of segregation.
It is necessary, he asserts, "to distinguish exactly the business of civil government from that of religion and to
settle the just bounds that lie between the one and the
other." The commonwealth, he continues, is "a society
of men constituted only for the procuring, the preserving,
and the advancing of their own civil interests," those
things belonging to this life. The jurisdiction of the
magistrate reaches only to these civil concernments." It
is "bounded and confined" to these things. It "neither can
nor ought in any manner to be extended to the salvation
of souls."[18] A church is defined in good Independent
fashion as "a voluntary society of men, joining together
of their own accord . . . in such a manner as they may
judge acceptable to . . . [God], and effectual to the salvation of their souls."

Nobody is born a member of any church; otherwise the
religion of parents would descend unto children by the same
right of inheritance as their temporal estates and everyone
would hold his faith by the same tenure as he does his lands,
than which nothing can be imagined more absurd. . . . No
man by nature is bound unto any particular church or sect,
but everyone joins himself voluntarily to that society in which
he believes he has found that profession and worship which
is truly acceptable to God.

In this respect, a church is like any other voluntary society
of men—"of philosophers for learning, of merchants for
commerce, or of men of leisure for mutual conversation."
Nor can the church be other than voluntary in character
for "men cannot be forced to be saved." It is "faith only
and inward sincerity" that "can procure acceptance with
God," and "no religion which I believe not to be true can
be either true or profitable unto me." As for a church,
"the right of making of its laws can belong to none but

the society itself, or at least, which is the same thing, to those whom the society by common consent has authorized thereunto." For the enforcement of these laws no force may be used, for "force belongs wholly to the civil magistrate." The only power at the disposal of a church, beyond "exhortations, admonitions, and advice," is for those of its members who are obstinate to be "cast out and separated from the society." Furthermore, since the power and authority of a church is purely "ecclesiastical,"

it ought to be confined within the bounds of the church, nor can it in any manner be extended to civil affairs; because the church itself is a thing absolutely separate and distinct from the commonwealth. The boundaries on both sides are fixed and immoveable. He jumbles heaven and earth together . . . who mixes these societies; which are in their original, end, business, and in everything, perfectly distinct and infinitely different from each other.

When this distinction between church and commonwealth —grace and nature—is clearly recognized, it becomes apparent that "liberty of conscience is every man's natural right."[19]

Williams' argument is identical. He also begins with the principle of segregation, asserting that there is a double ministry. "The one appointed by Jesus Christ in his church to gather, to govern, to receive in, cast out and order all the affairs of the church." The other, "a civil ministry or office, merely human and civil, which men agree to constitute . . . , and is as true and lawful in those nations . . . which never heard of the true God." Each bears an appropriate sword. The "sword of civil justice" is "for the defense of persons, estates, families, liberties of a city or civil state, and the suppressing of uncivil or injurious persons or actions by such civil punishment. It cannot, according to its utmost reach and capacity . . . , extend to spiritual and soul causes, spiritual and soul punishment, which belongs to that spiritual sword with two edges, the soul-piercing . . . Word of God." The end of civil government is "the commonweal or safety of . . . people in their bodies and goods" and it "extendeth no further than over the bodies and goods of the subject." It "hath no civil power over the soul, and therefore, say I, not in soul causes." Magistrates are "bounded to a civil work, with civil weapons or instruments, and paid or rewarded with civil rewards."[20] A true church is defined as being constituted of "living and believing stones," and any "church or company of believers (whether true or false) is like unto a body or college of physicians in a city, like unto a corporation, society, or company of . . . merchants, or any other society or company in London, which companies may hold their courts, keep their records, hold disputations, and in matters concerning their society may dissent, divide, break into schisms and factions." They may "wholly break up and dissolve into pieces and nothing, and yet the peace of the city not be in the least measure impaired or disturbed because . . . the city was before them and stands absolute and entire when such a corporation or society is taken down." The only power available to a church is exhortation, admonition, and exclusion from its own society. "Since God alone openeth the heart," God's people "must not be forced." Indeed, "forced worship stinks in God's nostrils," and Christ Jesus is not "pleased to make use of the civil magistrate to assist him in his spiritual kingdom." If the magistrate is permitted to intervene in matters of conscience, Williams asked, "what is this but to confound heaven and earth together . . . and to lay all upon heaps of confusion?" Whenever men "have opened a gap in the hedge or wall of separation between the garden of the church and the wilderness of the world," the garden has become a wilderness and all "civility" has been taken from the world.[21] Finally, with the principle of segregation clearly in mind, Williams insisted that the denial of freedom of conscience was a violation of "civil justice" because it exceeded the end and commission of civil government.[22]

Even in the realm of grace, however, neither Williams nor Locke believed that the magistrate's role need be wholly negative. Roger Williams affirmed that, beyond the "permission" and "protection" that the magistrate owes to the adherents of any religion, he owes to that faith which he believes to be true the more positive duty of public "approbation" ("a reverent esteem and honorable testimony") and "personal submission of his own soul to the power of the Lord Jesus."[23] The distinction, of course, was between the magistrate's office and his person. This theme was picked up and elaborated by Locke. Although "the care of souls does not belong to the magistrate," no man can be denied that "charitable care" for the souls of others which "consists in teaching, admonishing, and persuading." Thus "the magistrate may make use of arguments" to "draw the heterodox into the way of truth and procure their salvation," for "this is common to him with other men."

He may certainly do what becomes any good man to do. Magistracy does not oblige him to put off either humanity or Christianity. But it is one thing to persuade, another to command. . . . Every man has commission to admonish, exhort, convince another of error, and by reasoning to draw him into truth.

The magistrate's power does not extend "to the establishing of any articles of faith or forms of worship by the force of his laws."[24]

The exemption of articles of faith and forms of worship from the scope of the magistrate's authority, however, was not absolute, being qualified by both Williams and Locke. These limitations were grounded in the natural order and imposed by the end of civil government. "Laws respecting religion," said Williams, "may be such as merely concern the civil state, bodies and goods of such and such persons professing these and other religions," and where this is true, they are to be regarded as "merely civil." Furthermore, "if the church offend against the civil peace of the state by wronging the bodies or goods of any, the magistrate bears not the sword in vain to correct any or all the members of the church."[25] Locke was much more explicit and detailed than Williams at this point.

While government has nothing to do with the outward forms and rites of worship in general, Locke insisted that this does not grant such an exemption from the laws of the commonwealth that "promiscuous uncleanness" and other "heinous enormities"—such as "human sacrifice"— are to be permitted under color of religious worship. "These things are not lawful in the ordinary course of life, and therefore neither are they so in the worship of God." The general rule is this: "Whatsoever is lawful in the commonwealth cannot be prohibited by the magistrate in the church. Whatsoever is permitted unto any of his subjects for their ordinary use neither can nor ought to be forbidden by him to any sect of people for their religious uses."[26]

Locke brings articles of faith under similar scrutiny. While opinions do not ordinarily come within the competence of the magistrate, this does not mean that civil government is to be heedless of the practical consequences of some opinions that tend to destroy the very fabric of *all* society. The "all" is important. The concern is with those opinions that constitute a threat to any society, Christian or non-Christian. "The business of laws is not to provide for the truth of opinions," for "truth certainly would do well enough if she were left to shift for herself."[27] But some opinions are not purely speculative; they have practical consequences. And since the end of all government is "the safety and security of the commonwealth and every man's goods and person," account must be taken of these consequences. "No opinions contrary to human society or to those moral rules which are necessary to the preservation of civil society," Locke insisted, "are to be tolerated by the magistrate." Examples of opinions that "manifestly undermine the foundations of society and are therefore condemned by the judgment of all mankind" are such teachings as "men are not obliged to keep their promise" ("faith is not to be kept with heretics") and "princes may be dethroned by those that differ from them in religion" ("kings excommunicated forfeit their crowns and kingdoms"). These and similar doctrines "attribute unto the faithful" peculiar privileges, and their intent is only to "ask leave to be tolerated by the magistrate" until they find themselves strong enough "to seize the government and possess themselves of the estates and fortunes of their fellow subjects." Nor does that church have a right to be tolerated which delivers its adherents "to the protection and service of another prince." And lastly, "those are not to be tolerated who deny the being of God," for "promises, covenants, and oaths, which are the bonds of human society, can have no hold upon an atheist." The common feature of these several opinions which have no right to toleration is that they are destructive of all human society, and their condemnation is grounded on precepts derived from natural reason. Thus these opinions are brought within the scope of Locke's basic postulate that "the power of civil government relates only to men's civil interests, is confined to the care of the things of this world, and have nothing to do with the world to come."[28]

In *The Hireling Ministry,* Williams had adopted a similar position with regard to "offensive" opinions, distinguishing between those which savored of "impiety" and those which savored of "incivility." Christ, he insisted, "never called for the sword of steel to help the sword of the Spirit" against the first sort of offensive opinions, but "the second sort, to wit opinions of incivility . . . , are the proper object of the civil sword, according to that Magna Carta for the civil magistrate, *Rom. 13.*" Elsewhere in his writings, however, Williams notes the difference between sin or error and crime, and seems to imply that it is the consequence or act that alone should be punished. Locke, of course, makes the same point when he states that sins are not punishable by law but "only the injury done unto men's neighbors and to the commonwealth." But, as we have seen, Locke anticipates the injury that will be done by certain opinions and therefore justifies their condemnation by the magistrate.[29]

While Williams represented what was to become the dominant point of view in English Independency and Dissent, progress in this direction was faltering. The presuppositions were common to them all, but frequently there was confusion of counsel as to the precise application that was to be made. Even Williams was willing to grant that a magistrate could grant exemption from taxation to adherents of his own faith, because such an exemption harmed no one.[30] The author of *The Ancient Bounds* carried this principle somewhat farther. The general assumption was that the authority of the magistrate was limited to the Second Table of the Ten Commandments, but the author of *The Ancient Bounds* agreed with Locke and partially with Williams that the magistrate "may enter the vault even of those abominations of the First Table and ferret the devils and devil-worship out of their holes and dens so far as nature carries the candle before him." Such things as atheism, polytheism, and gross idolatry ("profane uncleanness"), the error of which may be demonstrated by "natural light," ought to be restrained. But in addition to this, he insisted that "blasphemy (which is against the Third Commandment and is a common nuisance to mankind) and the insolent profanation of the Lord's day (though the keeping of it be not obvious to nature's light) ought not to be suffered." The reason is that herein "no man's liberty is infringed, no man's conscience enthralled, truth not at all prejudiced or obstructed, while only manifest impiety and profaneness is excluded, and the peace of those that are better disposed procured, and scandal avoided by these negatives." These further limitations to toleration, as the author admitted, violated his own principle of segregation and left him open to the charge of inconsistency. The whole logic of his argument moved in the opposite direction.[31]

There were two fundamental concerns that gave urgency to the demand for toleration and liberty of conscience. Williams and the Independents generally were primarily concerned that the free operation of God's Spirit should not be impeded, and Williams insisted that the experience of "our own mistakes" and the "expectation of more light to come" does much to "sheath up the sword of persecution." But Williams also contended that toleration was necessary "for public peace and quiet sake" in order to avoid civil tumult and strife, and pointed out that "enforced uniformity (sooner or later) is the greatest occasion of civil war." By this "monstrous mingling of spiritual and civil," both the church and the state are reduced to "Babel's confusion and disorder."[32]

In Locke the stress upon the service of freedom to truth, though present, was muted. His major emphasis was upon the fact that attempts to impose religious uniformity had been the cause of almost all the wars that had troubled the life of Europe. "It is not the diversity of opinions (which cannot be avoided) but the refusal of toleration to those that are of different opinions . . . that have produced all the bustles and wars." Echoing the words of Williams, he declared that this has always been the consequence when men have "mixed together and confounded two things that are in themselves most different, the church and the commonwealth." If "each of them would contain itself within its own bounds, the one attending to the welfare of the commonwealth, the other to the salvation of souls, it is impossible that any discord should ever have happened between them."[33]

Both Williams and Locke agreed that persecution was foreign to the whole spirit of Christianity. "It is a mark of no true church," said Williams, "to procure the civil punishment of incorrigible, obstinate heretics and seducers." "The Christian church doth not persecute; no more than a lily doth scratch the thorns, or a lamb pursue and tear the wolves, or a turtle dove hunt the hawks and eagles, or a chaste and modest virgin fight and scratch like whores and harlots."[34] Locke, in similar fashion, insisted that a spirit of toleration is "the chief characteristical mark of the true church," since all evidences of intolerance are "marks of men striving for power and empire over one another than of the church of Christ." "A sweet religion, indeed," he commented, "that obliges men to dissemble and tell lies both to God and man for the salvation of their souls." In brief, toleration is so consonant both to the gospel of Jesus Christ and to "the genuine reason of mankind" that "it seems monstrous for men to be so blind as not to perceive the necessity and advantage of it."[35]

Both Locke and Williams rejected the notion that there could be a Christian state. Locke was explicit in stating that "there is absolutely no such thing . . . as a Christian commonwealth." Christ "instituted no commonwealth." He "prescribed unto his followers no new and peculiar form of government," nor did he put the "sword into any magistrate's hand with commission to make use of it in forcing men to forsake their former religion and receive his."[36] Williams was equally emphatic in asserting that magistracy receives "no addition of power from the magistrate's being a Christian, no more than it receives diminution from his not being a Christian; even as a commonwealth is a true commonwealth, although it have not heard of Christianity."

A Christian captain, Christian merchant, physician, lawyer, pilot, father, master, and (so consequently) magistrate, etc., is no more a captain, merchant, physician, lawyer, pilot, father, master, magistrate, etc. than a captain, merchant, etc. of any other conscience or religion.

Thus "a subject, a magistrate, may be a good subject, a good magistrate, in respect of civil or moral goodness . . . though godliness be wanting."[37]

To reject the notion of a Christian state, however, was not to affirm the notion of a secular state. To draw this conclusion would be to forget the principle of segregation upon which the whole structure was based. Although the language was sometimes confusing, the distinction was never between the religious and the nonreligious.[38] The two realms of nature and grace were equally under the government of God.[39] The distinction was between the ways in which the same God made himself and his will known, and between the ends that the two orders were designed to serve. In the one realm God was known through the light of nature that was common to all mankind. In the other realm, God was made known in Christ, an apprehension peculiar to the elect. The object of the one order was external peace. The object of the other order was internal peace. This distinction was most commonly expressed in terms of a distinction between the bodies and souls of men, but the claim of God was present in both categories and there was a degree of interpenetration. The moral demands of the realm of nature were not excluded from the life of grace, while, on the other hand, the illumination derived from God's special revelation in Christ taught the elect "to act in their several callings to an higher ultimate end, from higher principles, in a more heavenly and spiritual manner."[40]

Apart from his respectability, the great significance of Locke's *Letter concerning Toleration* was that it spelled out with clarity and persuasiveness the case for religious liberty that had been forged almost a half century earlier by Puritan divines. Its assumptions were Puritan assumptions, assumptions that were derived from Geneva and explicated by English Independents. By the time Locke wrote his letter, the logical implications of these assumptions had been accepted in England by all dissenting parties. In the Colonies, where they had not been subjected to the traumatic experience of the Clarendon Code, the progress of these same groups in this direction was somewhat more halting. Roger Williams had embarrassed the New England Congregationalists by basing his argument squarely upon their own presupposition. (For a brief statement that illustrates this point, see the *Queries of Highest Consideration* that Williams addressed to the Westminster divines.) And throughout the succeeding decades, New England Congregationalists continued to be embarrassed until they recast their practice by adopting a multiple establishment that permitted "the friendly cohabitation of all." By the time of the controversy over the Stamp Act, the story of the whole New England experiment—beginning with the landing of the Pilgrim Fathers in 1620—had been recast to portray it as a venture in which the goal was "liberty, both civil and ecclesiastical." Although practice was modified, no great adjustment in theory was necessary. The principle of segregation had always found expression in every pulpit, and the law of nature—as expounded, for example, in William Ames's *Conscience with the Power and Cases thereof* (1639)— had been a staple feature of instruction for successive generations of students at Harvard and Yale. The principles of fallibility and of consent were equally axiomatic, even though their implications had not always been clearly seen and practiced. Among the Presbyterians, who had profited from the lessons that had been taught them both by the troubles that had been encountered in Scotland and by their American experience, there was a parallel movement in the direction of a full acceptance of the position that had been spelled out by Roger Williams. As for Baptists and Quakers, they had originated as the radical wing of the Independent party and there is little evidence to indicate that they ever departed from the position that was being hammered out at the time of their birth.

The alliance between these pietistic heirs of John Calvin and the rationalists of the Revolutionary era in the struggle for liberty was far from strange. As Sidney E. Mead has pointed out, they were agreed on the same practical goal.[41] But they were also united ideologically, for the rationalists were operating within the context of the pietists' own categories. They had accepted the pietists' presuppositions, and they had adopted the pietists' arguments. Nor were the rationalists "secular" in their point of view. They still thought in terms of the claim of God in the natural order as it was made known to them by the light of nature. Even that most pietistically inclined of all the Puritans, Roger Williams, would have asked no more of them.

Chapter 7
John Witherspoon on Church and State
By James Hastings Nichols

In the development of the political thought and ethic of the Reformed churches, John Witherspoon is important as a representative rather than as a creative figure. He was not original in theology, philosophy, or political theory, but had decided opinions in all of these areas and great opportunity to make those opinions effective.

When John Witherspoon arrived in America from Scotland (1768) to preside over the college now known as Princeton, excitement was already mounting over the issues that were to ignite in less than a decade into the Revolution. In the American churches it was no longer a day for a revivalist like Whitefield or a philosophical theologian like Edwards, but a time for a man of affairs. Such a man was Witherspoon, aggressive, hardheaded, clear-minded, judicious, and courageous. Unlike his fellow college presidents of Yale and Harvard he actively engaged in politics, and Princeton became a chief center of agitation for the colonial cause. Witherspoon was elected, despite his earlier opposition to such activities for clergymen, to the colonial legislature and was sent from there as a delegate to the Continental Congress. There, as is well known, he was the only clerical signer of the Declaration of Independence. Reelected five times, he labored in the Congress through the war as one of its more influential and useful members. Among the more than one hundred congressional committees on which he served, two, the Board of War and the Committee on Secret Correspondence (Foreign Affairs), were of cardinal importance.

The British and the Tories thought Witherspoon a notable force against them. When the British troops captured the Reverend John Rosborough, they bayoneted him on the spot under the impression that they were disposing of the president of the College of New Jersey. And a Tory satirist devoted to the president some familiar lines:

> Meanwhile unhappy Jersey mourns her thrall
> Ordained by the vilest of the vile to fall;
> To fall by Witherspoon! . . .
> I'd rather be a dog than Witherspoon.[1]

Probably no other American clergyman of any denomination was more conspicuous or influential in the 1770's and 1780's in public affairs, and this was a day when the pulpit was still the chief molder of public opinion.

The body of ideas that Witherspoon championed was neither new nor distinctively American. The chauvinism of American historians has frequently led to such assertions. But the fathers of the American Revolution were really living on the intellectual capital of the English Revolution of the preceding century and added little to it. The political thought of the heirs of the Puritans was not broken in continuity from the days of Locke to those of Witherspoon, and the English nonconformists largely supported their American coreligionists during the Revolution. What was a defeated cause in England enlisted the effective majority of the American colonists. The Americans made it work, but added little to the theory. We might say not only was John Witherspoon not creative or original in these matters but neither were the American colonists in general. For originality we should have to go back to seventeenth-century England.

In the lectures given to his students at Princeton, Witherspoon showed himself in all essentials an exponent of John Locke's views on government and on toleration. "Society," wrote Witherspoon, "I would define to be an association or compact of any number of persons, to deliver up or abridge some part of their natural rights, in order to have the strength of the united body, to protect the remaining, and to bestow others." Society thus always presupposes an express or implied contract or agreement. From this "results this principle, that men are originally and by nature equal, and consequently free." The right of revolution is another consequence of the social contract. The right "that everyone should judge for himself in matters of religion" belongs to man by nature and is inalienable.[2]

This highly individualistic system of natural rights presupposes, of course, a more general theory of the law of nature, of principles of equity and order accessible to the natural reason and conscience of all men. How can one deny that the whole political ethic of the colonial representatives of the Reformed tradition was set in terms of natural law? Indeed, how can one deny this of the Reformers? To cite our best historian of Calvinism: "The assumption of some contemporary theologians that natural law has no place in the company of Reformed theology cannot be allowed to govern historical inquiry or to lead us to ignore, minimize, or evacuate of reality, the positive utterances on natural law scattered through the works of the Reformers." "Not one of the leaders of the Reformation assails the principle" of natural law. Natural law enters into the framework of their thought and is an assumption of their political and social teaching.

Specifically, Calvin adopts the natural law tradition, modifying it so as "to give increased emphasis to conscience and to reduce the medieval emphasis on reason. . . . Within the mundane society, natural law is not secondary but controlling—and this because it is not earthly but divine in origin, engraved by God on all men's hearts."[3]

Our special interest lies in Witherspoon's contribution to the formulation of policy for the American Presbyterian Church on church and state. The organizational structure of the old colonial synod of New York and Philadelphia had proved increasingly ineffective and unsatisfactory and after the war, steps were taken to reorganize. The result, as all know, was the General Assembly and the new Form of Government. In this reorganization Witherspoon was probably not so active or significant as John Rodgers of New York. But apparently Witherspoon did draft the preface that laid down the general principles. Among these are brief but important definitions concerning the relations of church and state.

Article I of the preface states the theological basis for religious liberty and continues:

> Therefore they consider the rights of private judgment, in all matters that respect religion, as universal and inalienable: they do not even wish to see any religious constitution aided by the civil power, further than may be necessary for protection and security, and, at the same time, be equal and common to all others.

This article has remained ever since the official position of American Presbyterianism regarding the relation of church and state. It will serve as text for the remainder of these remarks.

The formulation is twofold, the assertion of a universal inalienable right of private judgment in religion and the repudiation of special aid to churches by the civil power. The resemblance is striking to the two clauses of the First Amendment, drafted half a decade later by Witherspoon's student, James Madison. Under the First Amendment the Congress is enjoined from making any law respecting an establishment of religion or abridging its free exercise. In making the comparison, the intention is not to argue that the Preface to the Presbyterian Form of Government was a main source for the First Amendment. The point is simply that the Presbyterian Church had already defined its attitude to religious liberty on the one hand and to establishment or state aid on the other, before the First Amendment had even been dreamed of.

It will be noted, perhaps, that the term "separation of church and state" has not been employed. One reason is that it is not to be found in the Federal Constitution, the First Amendment, or the Preface to the Presbyterian Form of Government. It is a fairly satisfactory way of referring to the clauses repudiating special state aid or an establishment of religion, but these are only half of the relevant provisions, and, as will be argued, the less important half. Even in this case, a careful analysis should proceed from the language of the Constitution rather than from a popular unofficial summary term. There is some danger of starting from the abstract term "separation," which is not in the Constitution, and deducing conclusions therefrom as to what the Constitution intends. When Mr. Justice Frankfurter declared that "separation means separation, not something less," we must assume that as a justice of the Supreme Court he knew what he was doing. But for amateurs in the law, it seems more prudent to use the language of the Constitution in the explication of its meaning.

But before discussing the meaning of the First Amendment, we should make some further observations about the parallel Presbyterian formula. There, it seems clear, the separationist clause about no special state aid is less fundamental and important than the clause asserting religious freedom. The theological rationale, "God alone is Lord of the conscience," argues directly to religious liberty, only indirectly and instrumentally to separation. That the second clause on separation is to be read as an extension and application of the first is shown by the use of the adverb "even": "they do not *even* wish to see any religious constitution aided by the civil power."

A further argument is to be drawn from the fact that the American Presbyterian Church had been officially committed to religious liberty for half a century before the drafting of the Form of Government. It had not, however, been similarly formally committed to separation. In a memorable act of 1729 the colonial church had adopted as its own the Westminster Confession of Faith, together with a declaratory statement that radically revised the Confession in matters of church and state. As is well known, the Confession had originally been devised for the established church of the three kingdoms of England, Scotland, and Ireland. For them it provided that "the Civil magistrate . . . hath authority, and it is his duty, to take order . . . that all blasphemies and heresies be suppressed; all corruption and abuses in worship and discipline prevented or reformed, and all the ordinances of God duly settled, administered and observed."[4] In the same sense the Larger Catechism defined "tolerating a false religion" as a sin against the Second Commandment. Such was classical British Presbyterianism of the mid-seventeenth century.

When the colonial Presbyterians came to adopt the Confession, however, they rejected this whole theocratic view of church and state. The Synod declared unanimously in 1729 that they did not adopt the Westminster Confession to acknowledge in the civil magistrate a controlling power over synods, or "power to persecute any for their religion."[5] Since the Confession had asserted both powers explicitly and in terms, this explanation constituted radical surgery. A small body in both Scotland and America refused to modify the original intent of the Westminster Confession in this way and began a separate existence as the Church of the Covenanters. Colonial Presbyterianism, on the other hand, from its first official action in these matters, declared for the independence of the church from the state and for the religious liberty of all individuals. American Presbyterianism has never held any other view from first to last. The Form of Government of 1786 simply continued the position of the Adopting Act, elaborating and expanding it. Here John Witherspoon was reasserting the principles of Jonathan Dickinson in the matter. These principles were not forced on a reluctant church by secular pressures. They were held by conviction on theological grounds.

When we turn from religious liberty to the repudiation of special state aid, we enter a more complicated area. That section of Puritanism which championed religious liberty in the seventeenth century had divided into a right and left wing as regards the relation of the church to the state, a division that was important in Witherspoon's day and is also in ours.

The left wing held for a rigid separation of church and state, based on a theological compartmentalization of the spheres of creation (or nature) and of redemption (or grace). The state belonged to the sphere of nature and was to be shaped solely by natural law with no regard for Scripture or church. There could be no such thing as a "Christian state." There should be no religious tests for the franchise or an ecclesiastical intervention on political matters. The state, on the other hand, must respect the sphere of the church and redemption as outside its jurisdiction. Such was the scheme of Roger Williams in Rhode Island, and of John Lilburne and John Goodwin in old England. This became the mainstream of Baptist thought in England and the colonies and has remained so ever since.

A different but equally important pattern of thought had emerged at the Westminster Assembly, especially in the manifesto of the Congregational minority there. It was actually put into effect in the 1650's by Cromwell, but was then, of course, rejected at the Restoration of the Stuarts and the old episcopal establishment. This scheme fervently supported religious liberty as did the separationists. Cromwell's regime gave greater scope to religious liberty than any other major European state previously had done. But this tradition refused to give up the notion of the bearing of Christian revelation on political life. Cromwell conceived his government to be generically Christian, but without giving state aid to any ecclesiastic constitution preferentially. As he administered the parish system, benefices were held by ministers of Congregational, Presbyterian, Baptist, and Episcopal persuasions indifferently. To this extent it was a multiple establishment, based on the novel conception of a number of equal and independent denominations cooperating to shape a Christian nation. The state represented all collectively and equally on the basis of what was called "the common light of Christianity."

The state constitutions of Massachusetts, Connecticut, New Hampshire, and Maryland represented substantially this position in the 1780's. Public provision could be made for schoolteachers and religious ministrations of whatever denomination the several towns might wish, and in some cases at least, dissenting minorities were exempt from taxation. Nearly half of the states of the new republic maintained multiple establishments of this general type and the Congress provided something of the same sort for the Northwest Territory out of which five midwestern states have since been erected.

In Virginia, on the other hand, where the Anglican establishment had been less generous to dissenters than the Congregationalists of New England, it was the radical separationist view that triumphed under the leadership of Madison and Jefferson. And this Virginia struggle was the immediate background of the drafting of the First Amendment.

Where do the American Presbyterians fit into this picture? Although they rejected state support for church ministrations, their general outlook seems still to have been that of the Cromwellian "common light of Christianity." If we are to take Witherspoon's lectures on moral philosophy as a commentary on his preface to the Form of Government, the repudiation of special state aid does not imply a strict separationism of the Roger Williams or Baptist type. Whereas it is one of the most important duties of the civil magistrate to protect the rights of conscience, he is also, in Witherspoon's view, duty-bound to punish profanity and impiety. He should encourage piety by his own example, attending to public and private worship, avoiding swearing and blasphemy.[6] In Witherspoon's mind, the state was still called to give aid to Christianity in general in these ways. It was not expected to be neutral as between the religious and the irreligious. And, in his discussion of the system of state aid for public worship suiting the great body of citizens with full liberty for dissenters, Witherspoon observes mildly, "There is much reason in this." Clearly Witherspoon's devotion to the mechanism of separation is vastly less intense than his commitment to religious liberty. The main point is to secure freedom and nonpreferential treatment for all religious bodies and views. Separation was valued, not as an end in itself, but as a means to the end of religious liberty.

Witherspoon noted the problem raised by those who do not believe in religious liberty but use it to undermine it. Roman Catholicism was the prime instance. In Great Britain full religious liberty was denied to Roman Catholicism on three grounds. Roman Catholicism enjoined obedience to a foreign power, and one whose political orientation had often been opposed to British interests. It taught that persecution for religion was a religious obligation. And it denied a moral obligation to keep faith with heretics. Witherspoon was irenic in this connection. He noted that Roman Catholics denied the last charge (that they were taught it was not obligatory to keep faith with heretics). And as to the others, he observed that papists were tolerated in Holland without apparent damage to the state and that in Great Britain they were at least "connived at."

There are some interesting indications that even in constitutional law there may exist a relation between the two assertions of the First Amendment analogous to that which we have noted in eighteenth-century Presbyterian thought. The two notions of religious freedom and separation are not perhaps on the same level in law, any more than in political ethics. Nor are they two sides of the same coin.[7] Even in law, some distinguished jurists contend, separation is subordinate to religious freedom.

"The trouble with the 'separation' concept," argues Professor Katz, "is . . . that on debatable questions the analysis of this concept has little light to throw. . . . In determining the limits of constitutional separation, it is the concept of religious freedom which provides the criterion. The principle of church-state separation is an instrumental principle. Separation ordinarily promotes religious freedom; it is defensible so long as it does so, and only so long. . . . The basic American principle of church-state relations is not separation but religious liberty."[8]

By way of conclusion we should perhaps warn against using the precise position of Witherspoon or the founding fathers of the General Assembly as a static and final norm. It is doubtful whether their highly individualistic and unhistorical conceptions of either church or state can satisfy their successors. And changing times and circumstances require a redefinition of the relation of the two. But they may instruct us still by the fact that they dealt with the problem theologically and ecclesiastically rather than on mere pragmatic and political considerations. And again, although "the right of private judgment on religion" probably sounds to most Reformed churchmen today as a less than happy formulation for religious liberty, surely this is still the general ground from which the church must plot its course in relation to the state. Is there a better place to begin than with the declaration of the Westminster Assembly, "God alone is Lord of the conscience"?

Chapter 8
Abraham Lincoln and Calvinism
By William J. Wolf

I

The relation of Abraham Lincoln to a series of lectures on "Calvinism and the Political Order" is problematic. It could be easy to overstate this relationship by emphasizing too much the religious and political ideas in the theology of Puritanism. Yet without this background Lincoln's Christian statesmanship cannot be understood. Lincoln's own religious individualism and highly selective use of his religious and cultural inheritance should make any scholar suspicious of too simple a relationship.

The problem is further complicated by conflicting testimony about Lincoln's religious beliefs or the lack of them. Here the surest method of discerning truth from part truth or error is to use Lincoln's own writings and speeches as the control for evaluating the often conflicting and sometimes prejudiced testimony of his contemporaries. If nothing more were known of Lincoln than his Second Inaugural Address, it would still be possible to demonstrate his creative reinterpretation of Calvinism. Fortunately we are not reduced to so narrow a base for evidence.

Another problem is the definition of Calvinism itself. In this chapter it will be understood not simply as the chief points of the theology of John Calvin, but as the movement inaugurated by him. Calvinism had a fluid development through many stages: Scottish Puritanism, the

English Commonwealth, the New England theology of the seventeenth century, the relation to Deism in the era of the American Revolution and Constitutionalism, and finally the Calvinism of the American frontier in its conflicting sectarian forms. Professor John T. McNeill has a helpful summary of Calvinism. "It is characterized by a combination of God-consciousness with an urgent sense of mission. The Triune God, Sovereign Creator, Redeemer and Comforter, is an ever-present reality through both properity and disaster. Guilt is real, but it is submerged under grace. The Calvinist may be a very simple-minded theologian, but he is conscious that God commands his will and deed as well as his thought and prayer. This is what makes him a reformer and a dangerous character to encounter on moral and political issues. He is a man with a mission to bring to realization the will of God in human society."[1]

Sometimes the testimony of an expert who is unsympathetic to the very influences he discerns in his area of study is convincing in itself. No one will accuse Edmund Wilson of being partial to Calvinism. Yet Edmund Wilson writes of Lincoln's conception of the meaning of the Civil War:

"What *was* this interpretation? Like most of the important products of the American mind at that time, it grew out of the religious tradition of the New England theology of Puritanism."[2]

II

Let us now analyze briefly some of the institutional and personal religious influences operating on Lincoln. This will serve as introduction to the immeasurably more significant analyses of Lincoln's own writings and speeches.

In Indiana, Lincoln's parents and his sister Sally joined the Pigeon Creek Baptist Church. Thomas, the father, served as moderator and reconciler in matters of church discipline. "Hard-shell" Calvinism was the theology of this congregation, together with opposition to creeds other than the Bible itself. Born and raised among Predestinarian Baptists, Lincoln never became a Baptist, but he never ceased to be a predestinarian. We shall later examine the evidence for this. The scanty evidence in the New Salem period suggests a time of doubting and of rationalism for Lincoln. Benjamin Thomas writes of Lincoln's participation in the theological debates of New Salem: "Yet while he enjoyed them as a mental exercise, and while he eventually attained to a deep faith, emotionally the bitterness of sectarian prejudice must have been repellent to him, and was probably a cause of his lasting reluctance to affiliate with any sect."[3]

The evidence for the Springfield period is also not without conflicting testimony, but some of it can be summarized here in telegram style. Lincoln and Mary Todd were married by an Episcopal clergyman, the Rev. Charles Dresser. After the death of their son Edward, Mary and Abraham began to attend the First Presbyterian Church, whose Scottish-born minister, the Rev. James Smith (of Old School Presbyterianism), had helped them in their bereavement. Mary became a member, and the Lincolns had a special pew. There is, moreover, good evidence to the effect that Lincoln studied a book written by his minister, entitled *The Christian's Defense*. Anyone who takes the trouble to study this six hundred-page tome will find the author emphasizing such Calvinistic themes as the call, destiny, and responsibility of Israel. He also related these to American patriotism. Ninian W. Edwards, Lincoln's brother-in-law, reported that Lincoln told him, "I have been reading a work of Dr. Smith on the evidences of Christianity, and have heard him preach and converse on the subject and am now convinced of the truth of the Christian religion."[4]

Later, as president, Lincoln appointed Dr. Smith as American consul at Dundee. When his old pastor returned to his native Scotland, Lincoln described him in a note to Seward as "an intimate personal friend of mine."

In Washington the Lincolns attended the New York Avenue Presbyterian Church under its pastor Dr. Phineas Gurley, also an Old School divine. Thus Calvinism, judging now only in terms of external influences, came to Lincoln in its two classic forms: (1) the Baptist Independent tradition, which cherished the theology of Calvin without his polity and (2) the orthodox Presbyterian tradition embracing both Calvinistic doctrine and polity.

This is not to state that Lincoln accepted the system of Calvinism. It is merely to point out that Presbyterian preaching on such a theme as predestination may have helped him to give greater logical precision to fundamental insights acquired from his own study and use of the Bible.

III

It is important now to pass beyond environmental factors and the statements of others about his religion to the bedrock of his own utterance, there to detect the forms and emphases of Calvinism.

Our first solid evidence is the now-famous handbill discovered by Harry E. Pratt in 1941. It comes from the 1846 campaign for U.S. Congressman in which Lincoln's opponent was the colorful Methodist evangelist Peter Cartwright, twenty-four years his senior. Cartwright's forthrightness may be illustrated from a rebuke he addressed to a deacon who had offered a formal prayer: "Brother, three prayers like that would freeze hell over." Cartwright's friends had started a whispering campaign against Lincoln as an "infidel."

July 31, 1846

TO THE VOTERS OF THE SEVENTH CONGRESSIONAL DISTRICT

Fellow Citizens:

A charge having got into circulation in some of the neighborhoods of this District, in substance that I am an open scoffer at Christianity, I have by the advice of some friends

concluded to notice the subject in this form. That I am not a
member of any Christian Church, is true; but I have never
denied the truth of the Scriptures; and I have never spoken
with intentional disrespect of religion in general, or of any
denomination of Christians in particular. It is true that in
early life I was inclined to believe in what I understand is
called the "Doctrine of Necessity"—that is, that the human
mind is impelled to action, or held in rest by some power,
over which the mind itself has no control; and I have sometimes
(with one, two or three, but never publicly) tried to maintain
this opinion in argument. The habit of arguing thus however,
I have, entirely left off for more than five years. And I add
here, I have always understood this same opinion to be held
by several of the Christian denominations. The foregoing, is
the whole truth, briefly stated, in relation to myself, upon this
subject.

I do not think I could myself, be brought to support a man
for office, whom I knew to be an open enemy of, and scoffer
at, religion. Leaving the higher matter of eternal consequences, between him and his Maker, I still do not think any
man has the right thus to insult the feelings, and injure the
morals, of the community in which he may live. If, then, I
was guilty of such conduct, I should blame no man who should
condemn me for it; but I do blame those, whoever they may
be, who falsely put such a charge in circulation against me.[5]

"The Doctrine of Necessity" to which Lincoln alludes
is, of course, a philosophical rationalization of the Calvinist view of predestination. This is evident from his reference to its being "held by several of the Christian denominations." Lincoln may have stopped arguing philosophically about the doctrine of necessity, but he continued to
believe in predestination both in personal life and increasingly in the history of the nation. Let us examine this
characteristically Calvinist theme in one of his more mature documents. Discovered in his papers after his death,
this meditation had not been intended, said his secretaries
Nicolay and Hay, "to be seen of men." They assigned it
to late September, 1862, but the Rutgers editors have associated it with early September and his despair following
the second battle of Bull Run.

The will of God prevails. In great contests each party claims to act in accordance with the will of God. Both *may* be, and one *must* be wrong. God cannot be *for*, and *against* the same thing at the same time. In the present civil war it is quite possible that God's purpose is something different from the purpose of either party—and yet the human instrumentalities, working just as they do, are of the best adaptation to effect His purpose. I am almost ready to say this is probably true— that God wills this contest, and wills that it shall not end yet. By His mere quiet power, on the minds of the now contestants, He could have either *saved* or *destroyed* the Union without a human contest. Yet the contest began. And having begun, He could give the final victory to either side any day. Yet the contest proceeds.[6]

So strongly did Lincoln believe in this kind of predestination that he used this belief to protest against one of the five principles of Calvinism formulated at the Synod of Dort. He could not apparently accept the Calvinist theory of limited atonement. If we may trust the statement of his New Salem tutor Mentor Graham (and others also), Lincoln gave an absolute meaning to the phrase in I Cor. 15:22 "in Christ shall all be made alive." The ultimate salvation of all men through the universal efficacy of Christ's atonement would have been rank heresy to the regnant Calvinism of Lincoln's time, but his evaluation illustrates both independent judgment in matters religious and also his thoroughgoing use of predestination. Even his protest against orthodox Calvinism is expressed in the forms and themes of Calvinism.

Associated with the theme of God's will as utterly sov-ereign is the corollary of the nation as an "instrument" in God's hand and of Lincoln himself as an "instrument." This is a reaffirmation of that personal sense of responsi-bility in the context of the destiny of God's people that gave New England Puritanism its cutting edge.

The focus of our present interest is Lincoln as a Chris-tian statesman and Lincoln's religion as illuminating the spiritual center of American history. Let us allow Lincoln himself to sharpen our view. On that long, circuitous train ride from Springfield to Washington in 1861 the President-elect spoke many times about the nation as God's instrument and about himself as open to God's guidance and direction.

He spoke to the New Jersey legislators of his boyhood excitement in reading about the Revolutionary War and the promise in it for "all the people of the world for all time to come." Then he added: "I shall be most happy indeed if I shall be an humble instrument in the hands of the Almighty, and of this, his almost chosen people, for perpetuating the object of that great struggle."[7]

These two themes—"this Nation under God" and Lincoln as God's "humble instrument"—can be traced through the presidential years as they increase in depth and as they more and more penetrate each other.

The idea of national instrumentality, of openness to God's guidance, leads to a strong conviction that the democratic process of free discussion will ultimately express God's will. At Buffalo, Lincoln expressed the correlation as follows: "I must trust in that Supreme Being who has never forsaken this favored land, through the instrumentality of this great and intelligent people."[8] In the First Inaugural he spelled it out further in his plea for continued discussion:

Why should there not be a patient confidence in the ultimate justice of the people? Is there any better, or equal hope, in the world? In our present differences, is either party without faith of being in the right? If the Almighty Ruler of nations, with his eternal truth and justice, be on your side of the North, or on yours of the South, that truth, and that justice, will surely prevail, by the judgment of this great tribunal, the American people.[9]

The correlation between policy shaped by free discussion and the will of God is a legacy of radical or dissenting Puritanism either in its Baptist or Quaker phase. Professor James Nichols indicates its origin. "The most fundamental principle of liberal democracy, . . . the determination of policy by free discussion, is the secular reflection of the left-wing Puritan procedure of determining the counsel of the Holy Spirit in the Church."[10]

The circumstances surrounding Lincoln's decision to issue the preliminary proclamation of emancipation are fascinating in their religious overtones. We are carried back to the taking of covenants in New England and in Scotland; but, at the same time this is done amidst the most careful analysis of political possibilities and empirical realities. Lincoln had always believed slavery to be a moral wrong and had early risked his political future by calling it such in the Illinois Legislature, then predominantly southern in orientation. As President, however, he had felt that his sworn duty to uphold the Constitution obligated him to accept slavery where it already existed. Slowly he moved toward emancipation, convinced that he might legally free the slaves only as an act of military necessity.

Gideon Welles, Secretary of the Navy, has recorded in his diary the President's announcement to his Cabinet on September 22, 1862.

We had a special Cabinet meeting. The subject was the proclamation concerning emancipating slaves. . . . There were some differences in the Cabinet, but he had formed his own conclusions, and made his own decisions. He had, he said, made a vow, a covenant, that if God gave us the victory in the approaching battle [which had just been fought] he would consider it his duty to move forward in the cause of emancipation. We might think it strange, he said, but there were times when he felt uncertain how to act: that he had in this way submitted the disposal of matters when the way was not clear to his mind what he should do. God had decided this question in favor of the slave. He was satisfied it was right—was confirmed and strengthened by the vow and its results; his mind was fixed, his decision made; but he wished his paper announcing his course to be as correct in terms as it could be made without any attempt to change his determination. For that was fixed.[11]

The testimony is incontrovertible. Lincoln reached his decision about the timing of the proclamation in an immediate awareness of the presence of God. The solemn vow and covenant could become dangerous in the hands of a fanatic or even of a lesser man than Lincoln. The taking of vows and covenants is a characteristic feature of Calvinism. This practice was embedded in Lincoln's Biblical piety and came to him as part of the early religious heritage of the nation.

Lincoln revealed another side of his complex nature in his reply to two clergymen who presented him with a memorial demanding immediate emancipation:

I am approached with the most opposite opinions and advice, and that by religious men, who are equally certain that they represent the divine will. I am sure that either the one or the other class is mistaken in that belief, and perhaps in some respects both. I hope it will not be irreverent for me to say that if it is probable that God would reveal his will to others, on a point so connected with my duty, it might be supposed he would reveal it directly to me; for, unless I am more deceived in myself than I often am, it is my earnest desire to know the will of Providence in this matter. *And if I can learn what it is, I will do it!* These are not, however, the days of miracles, and I suppose it will be granted that I am not to expect a direct revelation. I must study the plain, physical facts of the case, ascertain what is possible and learn what appears to be wise and right. The subject is difficult, and good men do not agree.[12]

It is increasingly realized that although many of the composers of the Declaration of Independence and of the Constitution were Deists, they yet retained a deep suspicion of human nature that had been dramatized in the Calvinist emphasis on original sin. This suspicion about men explains the care of the Founding Fathers to distribute power over three branches of government and to provide a system of checks and balances. Lincoln was keenly aware of the ideological taint of self-interest that corrupts man's decisions. His strong prophetic sense of the injustice of slavery kindled in him an indignation at those clergymen who tried to defend the peculiar institution.

There is a fragment from the time of the classic debates against Douglas with a reference to a Dr. Ross, a minister in Alabama who wrote a pamphlet "Slavery as Ordained of God" in 1857.

> The sum of proslavery theology seems to be this: "Slavery is not universally *right*, nor yet universally *wrong*; it is better for some people to be slaves; and, in such cases, it is the will of God that they be such."
>
> Certainly there is no contending against the Will of God: but still there is some difficulty in ascertaining, and applying it, to particular cases. For instance we will suppose the Reverend Dr. Ross has a slave named Sambo, and the question is "Is it the will of God that Sambo shall remain a slave, or be set free?" The Almighty gives no audible answer to the question. . . . No one thinks of asking Sambo's opinion on it. So, at last, it comes to this, that Dr. Ross is to decide the question. And while he considers it, he sits in the shade, with gloves on his hands, and subsists on the bread that Sambo is earning in the burning sun. If he decides that God wills Sambo to continue a slave, he thereby retains his own comfortable position; but if he decides that God wills Sambo to be free, he thereby has to walk out of the shade, throw off his gloves, and delve for his own bread. Will Dr. Ross be actuated by that perfect impartiality which has ever been considered most favorable to correct decisions?
>
> But, slavery is good for some people!!! As a *good* thing, slavery is strikingly peculiar, in this, that it is the only good thing which no man ever seeks the good of, for *himself*.
>
> Nonsense! Wolves devouring lambs, not because it is good for their own greedy maws, but because it is good for the lambs!!![13]

One of the greatnesses of Lincoln was the way he held to strong moral positions without the usual accompaniment of self-righteousness or smugness. He expressed this rare achievement provisionally in his humor and in an ultimate way in his religious evaluations. To the Pennsylvania delegation that congratulated him after the inaugu-

ration he said, urging forbearance and respect for differences of opinion between the states, "I would inculcate
this idea, so that we may not like Pharisees, set ourselves
up to be better than other people."[14]

Lincoln held the nation under God's judgment. He was
very far removed from a current type of piety that drags
God in by the back door in the last paragraph. A southern
newspaper gave wide publicity to one of Lincoln's en-
counters with a clergyman in a visiting delegation. The
minister said he hoped "the Lord was on our side." When
Lincoln rejoined, "I don't agree with you," all were surprised. The President made it clearer. "I am not at all
concerned about that, for I know the Lord is always on
the side of the right. But it is my constant anxiety and
prayer that I and this Nation should be on the Lord's
side."[15]

Such perspective and detachment from self-justification
is the fruit of the conviction that God is Lord of this
universe. In his proclamation after the disaster of Bull
Run in July, 1861, he expressed his belief in God as ruler
of the nations. "It is fit and becoming in all people, at all
times, to acknowledge and revere the supreme government of God: to bow in humble submission to His chas-
tisements; to confess and deplore their sins and transgres-
sions in the full conviction that the fear of the Lord is the
beginning of wisdom. . . . It is peculiarly fit for us to
recognize the hand of God in this terrible visitation, and
in sorrowful remembrance of our own faults and crimes as
a nation and as individuals, to humble ourselves before
Him, and to pray for His mercy."[16]

Not only could Lincoln in his proclamations express
God's punishments for the sins of the nation but also he
could express national thanksgiving in a religious dimension of depth. Lincoln was the first President to declare
Thanksgiving a national holiday in 1863. A study of these
proclamations would underscore Lincoln's themes:—the
nation devoted to a cause larger than its own life, grateful-

ness in detail for special providences, penitence as the proper approach of man to God, and the vocation of the American people in the new Promised Land. Here is a paragraph from the 1864 Proclamation.

. . . a day of Thanksgiving and Praise to Almighty God, the beneficent Creator and Ruler of the Universe, and I do further recommend to my fellow-citizens aforesaid that on that occasion they do reverently humble themselves in the dust and from thence offer up penitent and fervent prayers and supplications to the Great Disposer of events for a return of the inestimable blessings of Peace, Union and Harmony throughout the land, which it has pleased Him to assign as a dwelling place for ourselves and for our posterity throughout all generations.[17]

The key to Lincoln's faith is the Bible; and it would not be an exaggeration to say that the glasses through which he read Scripture had the lens of Calvinism in them. Here is one of his evaluations of the Bible:

In regard to this Great Book, I have but to say, it is the best gift God has given to man. All the good the Savior gave to the world was communicated through this book. But for it we could not know right from wrong. All things most desirable for man's welfare, here and hereafter, are to be found portrayed in it.[18]

The Second Inaugural is the climax of Lincoln's religious development. In it he gave the theme of "this Nation under God" its most powerful expression. Earlier, in the proclamation after Bull Run, he had urged the nation to see the hand of God in the terrible visitation of war. Increasingly he defined the theological issue in the conflict. His papers and letters show his belief that God willed America to be the bearer of new freedom to all men everywhere. The Puritan background of Lincoln's confidence in American destiny under God had become rationalized in the eighteenth and nineteenth centuries into the dream of world democracy with the original religious perspective rapidly disappearing into the distance. With his incisive logic Lincoln gave definition to America's hope for democracy in terms compelling to his contemporaries, but he also sustained that vision in its original religious rootage and reference to God's will. The religious interpretation was organic and fundamental.

Lincoln interpreted the slavery issue in terms of the Old Testament prophets. His Puritan forebears would have called it "a discerning of the signs of the times." As Lincoln analyzed God's intention to lead men into larger freedom and appropriated to his use the language of the Declaration of Independence and the sayings of the Founding Fathers he came, in the context of events, to regard slavery as a contradiction of God's will. This defiance of God's justice had been built into the life of the nation and was therefore subject to God's judgment.

The long, unhappy debates over the slavery issue had weakened the nation and made it seem hypocritical to aspiring men in other countries. For somewhat more than the last year of his life Lincoln understood the tragedy and suffering of the Civil War as God's judgment upon this evil and as punishment to bring about its removal. The judgment fell upon both sides, for slavery was a national and not merely a sectional evil. The North had also prospered from the cheap raw materials that slave labor fed into its factories. It was conceivable to Lincoln that a just God might allow the war to continue "until all the wealth piled by the bondmen's 250 years of unrequited toil shall be sunk." In the severe language of Scripture, Lincoln held the nation under judgment: "The judgments of the Lord are true and righteous altogether."

But the judgments of God have as their purpose the reformation of his people. The renewal of an America newly dedicated to the increase of freedom had been his theme at Gettysburg and must be understood as the implied correlative here of the emphasis upon judgment.

The leaven that is at work in this address and which carries the analysis of judgment beyond that of an Amos or a Jeremiah is expressed in the Savior's warning about the peril of judging. It is also present in the Scriptural paraphrase of the Savior's summary of the law and of Paul's famous chapter on love that Lincoln achieves in his phrases "With malice toward none; with charity for all." The disclaimer of human judgments does not lead, however, to irresolution in action. The very opposite is the case. Understanding the perspective of two antagonists before the judgment seat of God and thereby freed from the tyranny of self-righteous fanaticism, there comes to Lincoln the resource of "firmness in the right as God gives us to see the right."

This document is one of the most astute pieces of theology ever written. It may seem strange to call Lincoln a theologian, for he was obviously not one in any technical sense. There are many profundities in the Christian religion that he never did illuminate; but in the area of his vision he saw more keenly than anyone since the inspired writers of the Bible. He knew he stood under the living God of history.

The Second Inaugural illuminates the finiteness of man when in sincerity men embrace opposite courses of action under the conviction that each is responsive to God's will. "Both read the same Bible, and pray to the same God: and each invokes His aid against the Other."

There is a fanaticism in men that blinds them to the truth of their position, increases their self-righteousness, and isolates them from their fellows. It is the fallacy of supposing that a sincere intention to do God's will guarantees that what I sincerely do is the will of God. Lincoln could detach himself from the element of pretense in the idealistic claims made by both sides. In his earlier meditation on the divine will Lincoln opened up horizons beyond the simple but all too common analysis that one side is right and the other wrong. Both could not be right. Each might be partly right and partly wrong and God might use both sides as his instruments to effect a result not foreseen by either side. Lincoln argues that this was the case with the Civil War. "Only God can claim it," he once said, thereby stating that the complexities of historical events are so involved that man cannot claim infallible insight for his own interpretations. Lincoln expressed this again in his own comments on the Second Inaugural in a letter to Thurlow Weed:

I expect the latter to wear as well as—perhaps better than —anything I have produced; but I believe it is not immediately popular. Men are not flattered by being shown that there has been a difference between the Almighty and them. To deny it, however, in this case, is to deny that there is a God governing the world: It is a truth which I thought needed to be told; and as whatever of humiliation there is in it, falls most directly on myself, I thought others might afford for me to tell it.[19]

Knowing that God and not Lincoln would have the final word in the dilemma of the two contestants at prayer, he could yet venture provisional judgments and act resolutely in their light. "It may seem strange that any men should dare to ask a just God's assistance in wringing their bread from the sweat of other men's faces."

He could appreciate the sincerity of his foe although he believed him wrong, but because of his religious perspective he could deal magnanimously and forgivingly without assuming the self-righteousness of the victor.

IV

Lincoln's religious analysis of the nation's history is as relevant today as it was when he painfully developed it. One has only to substitute the phrase "segregation" for Lincoln's word "slavery" and his theological analysis becomes luminous. America stands today among the nations of the world as the self-professed defender of democracy in areas that are being progressively inundated by undemocratic governments. Our professed defense of the right of all men everywhere to be free sounds increasingly hollow to multitudes in Asia and Africa because of our continuing racial discrimination at home. If the rising colored peoples of the world turn from democracy to communism partly because of our racialism, the security of America will become a very frail thing. And yet we must repeat Lincoln's quotation from the psalms: "The judgments of the Lord are true and righteous altogether."

To a religious understanding of the nation's destiny that is as meaningful today as for the crisis of the Civil War, Lincoln adds a dynamic for responsible action that is equally helpful. Lincoln could concentrate on practical actions needed to restore the Union because he was free of the determination to punish the South. A Christian statesmanship rooted in reconciliation marks the address he made on the evening of April 11, 1865, his last public utterance. He appealed to the people to support his principles and action for reconstruction. "Let us all join in doing the acts necessary to restoring the proper practical relations between these States and the Union; and each forever after, innocently indulge his own opinion whether, in doing the acts, he brought the States from without, into the Union, or only gave them proper assistance, they never having been out of it."[20]

The problems of national reconciliation in a spirit of forgiveness were uppermost in his mind when the bullet struck him on Good Friday. He carried to his death another item of unfinished business mentioned four days before in this last speech. "Him from whom all blessings flow, must not be forgotten. A call for a national thanksgiving is being prepared, and will be duly promulgated."[21]

Lincoln was a Biblical Christian, or to be still more precise, a Biblical prophet who saw his country as "God's almost chosen people" called to world responsibility and himself as "an instrument of God" responsible "to the American people, to the Christian world, to History, and on final account to God."[22]

The Second Inaugural reads like a supplement to the Bible. In it there are fourteen references to God, four quotations from Genesis, Psalms, and Matthew, and other allusions to Scriptural teaching.

In it are reflected many of the Calvinist themes related to political order that we have observed in his other documents—God as guiding the nation's history, the solemn responsibility for individual and nation to learn God's will in order to become his instruments, the solemn taking of vows and covenants with respect to historical events under a faith in special providences, national humiliation, and thanksgiving as the fitting responses to disaster and victory. Yet Lincoln is no mere rehabilitator of Calvinist themes. He creatively remolds them, deepening them and universalizing them until all mankind is included and brought into a mutual relationship of forbearance.

Frederick Denison Maurice, the English thinker and educator, within three months of the Second Inaugural in a little-known letter made probably the most astute evaluation ever made of the address. It underscores both the positive and negative relationships between Lincoln and Calvinism.

I regard Lincoln's inauguration speech as the grandest return . . . to the theocracy of the Pilgrim Fathers that I have seen anywhere. I always hoped that might be the effect of the war on the best Americans. I never dreamed of seeing it expressed officially in such language as that. And it was not merely the old Calvinistic theocracy—the divinity minus humanity. In so far as it recognized the divine vengeance for the wrongs of the colored race, it implied a Christ as Head of the human race.[23]

Chapter 9
Woodrow Wilson:
Presbyterian in Government
By Arthur S. Link

Nothing could be more appropriate in a volume of essays on Calvinism and the political order than a discussion of Woodrow Wilson and his life of Christian faith in the world of politics. He stands preeminent among all the inheritors of the Calvinist tradition who have made significant contributions to American political history. Indeed, he was the prime embodiment, the apogee, of the Calvinist tradition among statesmen of the modern epoch. Every biographer of Wilson has said that it is impossible to know and understand the man apart from his religious faith. His every action and policy was ultimately informed and molded by the Christian insight that was given him.

One word of qualification and explanation is necessary at the beginning of this paper. Woodrow Wilson was first a Christian and secondarily a Presbyterian; that is, his faith was that faith which God gives to the one holy catholic church. He was, moreover, an ecumenically-minded Christian. As an undergraduate at Princeton University, and later as professor and president, he took active part in the interdenominational Philadelphian Society, the Y.M.C.A., and the World Student Christian Movement. As Governor of New Jersey and President of the United States, when his influence and interests had wider scope, he played as active a role as possible in the work of such groups as the Sunday School Union and the Federal Council of Churches of Christ in America. In death he sleeps in a crypt in an Episcopal cathedral. Insofar as the voluminous evidence of his life can show, he had no sectarian pride or consciousness; nor, for that matter, did he ever show any trace of antipathy toward other Protestants, Roman Catholics, and Jews. This was true, one would like to believe, because Wilson was a faithful Presbyterian. But saying this does not get this writer off a very sharp methodological hook—the difficulty, almost impossibility, of discriminating between those influences in Wilson's life and thought that are God's gift to his one church and those that might be defined as being more or less an inheritance of the Calvinist tradition. This lecture will attempt to concentrate on the latter, but there will be many occasions when readers might rightly substitute the word "Christian" when they read "Presbyterian."

I. WOODROW WILSON, PRESBYTERIAN LAYMAN

The sheer weight of historical evidence tempts one to say that Wilson was predestined to be a Presbyterian. His ancestors in Scotland and Ireland, insofar as we know from scanty family records, had been Presbyterians since the Reformation. His mother's father, Thomas Woodrow, was a Scottish Presbyterian minister who moved to the New World in the early nineteenth century and after a brief sojourn in Canada, settled in Ohio. His mother's brother, the Reverend Doctor James Woodrow, was long a professor at the Columbia Theological Seminary—until his opponents finally obtained his dismissal from his chair because he taught theistic evolution. His father, the Reverend Doctor Joseph Ruggles Wilson, was not only a minister but also a leader in the Southern Presbyterian Church and was Permanent Clerk and Stated Clerk of the General Assembly of that body from 1861 to 1898 and sometime professor at the Columbia and Southwestern Theological Seminaries.

Woodrow Wilson was born in the Presbyterian manse in Staunton, Virginia, on December 28, 1856, and grew

up in manses in Augusta, Georgia, Columbia, South Carolina, and Wilmington, North Carolina. Thus he had, as he
once put it, "the unspeakable joy of having been born and
bred in a minister's family." It was a secure, tightly-knit
family dominated by a strong-willed father who valued
education along with faith. Young Woodrow grew up on
family worship, Bible reading, study of the Shorter Catechism, and stories of Scottish Covenanters. As he later
said in a speech in London on his sixty-second birthday,
"The stern Covenanter tradition that is behind me sends
many an echo down the years."[1] Admitted to the membership of the First Presbyterian Church of Columbia on
July 5, 1873, he also grew up in the bosom of the church,
imbibing unconsciously its traditions and faith. He shared
in its work as his father's right-hand man in pastoral
calling, in the business of the *North Carolina Presbyterian,*
which his father edited for a time, and in preparing the
minutes of the General Assembly.

Such an inheritance laid strong foundations for faith in
mature life. "*My* life," he told a friend when he was
President of the United States, "would not be worth living if it were not for the driving power of religion, for
faith, pure and simple. I have seen all my life the arguments against it without ever having been moved by
them. . . . There are people who *believe* only so far as
they *understand*—that seems to me presumptuous and sets
their understanding as the standard of the universe. . . . I
am sorry for such people."[2] It was true, and Wilson was
apparently never buffeted by strong winds, much less
storms, of doubt. His faith found expression, among other
ways, in family worship, daily prayer and Bible-reading,
and, above all, active church membership. He and his
family were members, successively, of the Bryn Mawr
Presbyterian Church, the Congregational Church of Mid-
dletown, Connecticut, the Second Presbyterian Church of
Princeton, and the First Presbyterian Church of the same
town. He was ordained a Ruling Elder in 1897 and served
on the sessions of both Princeton churches.[3]

Wilson and his wife moved their membership to the Central Presbyterian Church when they went to Washington in 1913, thus resuming intimate relationship with the denomination in which they had both been reared. It was a small congregation, and Wilson loved its simple service—it took him back, he said, to "the days when I was a boy in the South"[4]—and the courtesy of the members in permitting him to worship quietly. "I have been to church," he wrote, for example, one Sunday in 1913, "in a dear old-fashioned church such as I used to go to when I was a boy, amidst a congregation of simple and genuine people to whom it is a matter of utter indifference whether there is a [social] season or not."[5] He attended as regularly as possible until 1919, when illness confined him to his home, and he showed his concern in ways large and small. He also developed a warm friendship with the church's pastor, Dr. James H. Taylor, that lasted until Wilson's death in 1924.[6]

Wilson was one of the most thoughtful and articulate Christians of his day. He spoke with increasing perception and power on subjects ranging from problems of the ministry and Christian education to problems of the rural church in a changing society.[7] He was, additionally, a pulpit preacher of moving eloquence and great evangelical fervor. He preached only in the Princeton Chapel, and all but one of his sermons have remained unpublished and consequently generally unknown. They were among the greatest speeches that he ever delivered.[8]

Having established Wilson's credentials, so to speak, as a Christian and Presbyterian, let us now turn more directly to the subject of this essay and see how faith influenced Wilson as a politician and statesman.

II. Morality and Politics

It is fairly common knowledge that Woodrow Wilson was an honorable man. His integrity was as considerable as his personal ethics were lofty. Before he entered politics he had already given abundant evidence of integrity as president of Princeton when he risked serious decline in enrollment by greatly elevating academic standards and refusing to change policies in order to curry favor with alumni or potential donors. He was the same kind of man in politics. He was incapable not only of outright corruption but also of the more subtle and dangerous forms of corruption such as acceptance of political support when he knew that strings were attached. For example, he nearly wrecked his chances for the presidential nomination in 1912 by literally telling William Randolph Hearst, whom he abhorred, to go to hell when Hearst offered his support. He resisted the most insidious temptation that can corrupt a leader in a democracy, that of following policies simply because a majority of people wanted him to follow them. For example, he refused to yield to public clamor for a march through Germany in the autumn of 1918 and proceeded to negotiate for an end to the World War. When a senator warned him that he would be destroyed if he did not yield to public demand, he replied: "So far as my being destroyed is concerned, I am willing if I can serve my country to go into a cellar and read poetry the remainder of my life. I am thinking now only of putting the U.S. into a position of strength and justice."[9] More important, he refused later, in 1919 and 1920, to accept the Lodge reservations to the Versailles Treaty and thereby made defeat of ratification inevitable, even though many of his friends, party leaders, and leaders of public opinion in the country urged him to accept ratification on Lodge's terms. He simply could not do something that he believed constituted both a rank betrayal of America's plighted word and stultification of his own creation, the League of Nations. There is no need to labor the obvious. Let it suffice to say that Wilson set an example of morality in politics excelled by few other American statesmen.

It is more important to talk about the wellspring of Wilson's morality—his belief, undoubtedly sharpened and defined by the Calvinist emphasis, that God governs the universe through moral law, and that men and nations are moral agents accountable to God and transgress that law at the peril of divine judgment. This theme runs through virtually all his political speeches. But to stop at this point would be to repeat the common mistake of saying, at least implying, that Wilson was simply a moralist who lived rigidly by rules, with all the inevitable consequences of this way of life. Wilson, in fact, had a very sophisticated understanding of Christian ethics. He believed firmly, deeply, in moral law and judgment, but he understood them also in the light of God's love and reconciling work in Jesus Christ. Moreover, he believed that morality and character were by-products of obedience, like Christ's own obedience, and that Christ alone gives individuals power to live righteously by enabling them truly to love one another. He said these things many times, but nowhere more movingly than in his baccalaureate sermon at Princeton in 1905:

And so the type and symbol is magnified,—Christ, the embodiment of great motive, of divine sympathy, of that perfect justice which seeks into the hearts of men, and that sweet grace of love which takes the sting out of every judgment. . . . He is the embodiment of those things which, not seen, are eternal,—the eternal force and grace and majesty, not of character, but of that which lies back of character, obedience to the informing will of the Father of our spirits. . . . [In Christ] we are made known to ourselves,—in him because he is God, and God is the end of our philosophy; the revelation of the thought which, if we will but obey it, shall make us free, lifting us to the planes where duty shall seem happiness, obedience liberty, life the fulfillment of the law.

And in his address to the Pittsburgh Y.M.C.A. in 1914, as follows:

I have always been very impatient of processes and institutions which said that their purpose was to put every man in the way of developing his character. My advice is: Do not think about your character. . . . Character is a by-product, and any man who devotes himself to its cultivation in his own case will become a selfish prig.

Wilson suffered the plagues of sin and death, like the rest of mortals. He had a powerful ego and drive toward dominance. He had a tendency to identify his own solutions with the moral law. He often sounded like a moralizer. But in forming judgment, one must look at Wilson's entire career in politics, not just at the episodes that support a particular interpretation. The record shows a man committed very deeply to fundamental Christian affirmations about moral law, but also enormously flexible about details and methods, so long as they did not violate what he thought was right. One cannot follow Wilson day by day, even hour by hour, without concluding that here, indeed, was a man who tried to live by faith rather than by rules, in meeting complex moral problems. As he put it in his baccalaureate sermon in 1905:

But the standard? It is easy enough to talk of assessing moral values and of increasing the stock of good in the world, but what is good and what is evil, for us individually and for the world? May we not determine that deep question by our experience, candidly interrogated and interpreted,—by the peace, the ardour, the satisfaction our spirits get from our own days and their tasks,—by the tonic health we get from one course of action, the restlessness, the bitterness, the disappointment and weariness we get from another? . . . You shall not find happiness without health, and health lies in the constant rectification of the spirit, its love of the truth, its instinctive sincerity, its action without fear and without corruption of motive, its self-sufficing energy and independence. It is God's power in the heart. It is the spirit's consciousness of its immediate connection with his will and purpose. It is his saving health, which must be known among all nations before peace will come and life be widened in all its outlooks.

This was the life of freedom from the law that Wilson lived.

III. GOD'S PROVIDENCE AND THE LORDSHIP OF JESUS CHRIST

Wilson was most obviously a Calvinist in his emphasis upon the majesty and sovereignty of God. He literally stood in awe of the Almighty One. He was not a prig, and he occasionally used words that some Presbyterians would not approve. But using the name of God lightly was to him blasphemy against divine majesty. His daughter, Mrs. Eleanor Wilson McAdoo, has told the present writer about his fearsome reaction when she once repeated a ditty that took liberties with God's name. This is said merely as illustration of Wilson's consciousness, manifested in numerous other ways, that he stood constantly in the presence of a jealous God.

This same God was, in Wilson's view, not only the Lord of individuals but also the Lord of history, ruler of men and nations, who turned all things to his own purpose. "The idea of an all merciful God," Wilson's brother-in-law once said, "was, I believe to him, a piece of soft sentimentality."[10] This did perhaps characterize Wilson's earlier understanding of God's sovereignty as it had been influenced by his father's stern Calvinism. But it was not Wilson's mature understanding of the sovereign Lord of history. At least by the early 1900's he had come to a new understanding—that men know God truly only through Jesus Christ. God's saving work in history is most clearly revealed in his work of reconciliation through Christ who is also the Lord of the ages. God's providence did not end with the once-for-all revelation. In his triune nature he has been constantly at work in the affairs of men, shaping, directing, and controlling history in order to achieve his purpose of advancing justice, righteousness, and human welfare. Men might, often do, try to thwart God's saving work. It does not matter. They are contemptible, futile, and impotent. It is man's duty to apprehend God's purposes and then cheerfully to cooperate.

"The providence of God," Wilson told a Trenton Sunday school convention in 1911, "is the foundation of affairs." In the next breath he linked providence to revelation, saying: "Only those can guide, and only those can follow, who take this providence of God from the sources where it is authentically interpreted. . . . He alone can rule his own spirit who puts himself under the command of the Spirit of God, revealed in His Son, Jesus Christ, our Savior. He is the captain of our souls; he is the man from whose suggestions and from whose life comes the light that guideth every man that came into the world."

Wilson had this to say in his address on the Bible in 1911 about the irresistibility of God's providential work:

The man whose faith is rooted in the Bible knows that reform cannot be stayed, that the finger of God that moves upon the face of the nations is against every man that plots the nation's downfall or the people's deceit; that these men are simply groping and staggering in their ignorance to a fearful day of judgment; and that whether one generation witnesses it or not the glad day of revelation and of freedom will come in which men will sing by the host of the coming of the Lord in His glory, and all of those will be forgotten—those little, scheming, contemptible creatures that forget the image of God and tried to frame men according to the image of the evil one.

There was power in faith such as this. For Wilson it meant, when plans were succeeding, the strength and joy that come from conviction that one is doing God's work in political affairs. It also brought courage and hope in the time of his great adversity, when the Senate wrecked his work at Versailles, and as he thought, the best hope for peace in the world. "I feel like going to bed and staying there," he told his physician, Dr. Cary T. Grayson, after he had received word that the Senate had rejected the treaty for a second time. But later in the night he had Dr. Grayson read II Cor. 4: 8-9, and then he said, "If I were not a Christian, I think I should go mad, but my faith in God holds me to the belief that He is some way working out His own plans through human perversities and mistakes."[11] Later, in the last public speech that he ever made, he reiterated his unshaken faith: "I am not one of those who have the least anxiety about the triumph of the principles I have stood for. I have seen fools resist Providence before, and I have seen their destruction, as will come upon these again, utter destruction and contempt. That we shall prevail is as sure as that God reigns."[12]

To be sure, faith like this carried obvious dangers, the principal one being the temptation to believe that what the self wants to do is what God commands, and that one's opponents are not only mistaken but of evil heart and mind. But all Christian statesmen have to run such dangers. And if Wilson succumbed at times, he never forgot for long that he was a servant of Jesus Christ, and that the final judgment belongs to God. As he once said in a reflective moment about men with whom he disagreed, "While we are going to judge with the absolute standard of righteousness, we are going to judge with Christian feeling, being men of a like sort ourselves, suffering the same temptations, having the same weaknesses, knowing the same passions: and while we do not condemn, we are going to seek to say and to live the truth."[13] Wilson even came to accept defeat of American membership in the League of Nations as God's decision, saying humorously, "Perhaps God knew better than I did after all."[14]

IV. Presbyterianism and an Ordered Political System

It is a great temptation to an admirer of the Presbyterian form of government to say that Woodrow Wilson was profoundly influenced by the constitutional structure of the Presbyterian Church. He believed very ardently in representative government and spent a good part of his adult life, both as scholar and politician, trying to make it work more effectively in the United States. He was forever writing constitutions for college debating societies, and he crowned this activity by writing one for the government of the world. He knew the Presbyterian system as well as any statesman this country has ever produced, and he undoubtedly admired it. But there is not a shred of evidence to suggest that his study and practice of the Presbyterian system influenced his thinking about a secular political order, although there is a great deal of evidence that English and American political theorists and practitioners influenced him strongly in this field. Thus we have to conclude that the evidence does not warrant any conclusions about the impact of the Presbyterian system upon Wilson's political thought.

V. Christianity, Social Conscience, and Political Action

The most remarkable thing about Wilson as a political leader was the change that occurred in his thinking about the functions of government. Even more remarkable was the way Wilson's views on government paralleled his thinking about the Christian's duty toward his fellowman. This was more than mere coincidence. Wilson's views about the role that government should play were inseparable, indeed, stemmed directly, from his growing understanding of Christian social and political duty.

Wilson grew up during the high tide of individualism in the Western world. His political heroes were the English devotees of *laissez faire*, Cobden, Bright, and Gladstone, and the earlier but equally conservative Burke. He studied with some admiration British and American classical economists, including Adam Smith, Malthus, Ricardo, and Amasa Walker. He inherited from scholastic Presbyterianism its pietism, individualism, and almost total rejection of organized social action either by religious or political communities. It is difficult to separate the strands, for pietism, the gospel of wealth, social Darwinism, classical economics, and *laissez faire* in government were all more or less based on the same assumptions and reinforced one another. At the risk of making a crude and partially inaccurate generalization, we can say that Wilson, like most eastern academic people during his day, did not seriously question prevailing assumptions. He admired rich men and captains of industry and their political allies like Grover Cleveland and William McKinley. He had ill-disguised contempt for the Populists, William Jennings Bryan, and other tribunes of the discontented. He seems to have been oblivious of the great movement to reawaken Christian social conscience that began in an organized way in the 1870's and was beginning to leaven American religious thought and life by the 1890's. This was true even as late as the first decade of the twentieth century, when Wilson was president of Princeton University. He gained what little political fame he then enjoyed as a critic of Bryan and Theodore Roosevelt and advocate of very cautious solution of economic and political problems.

Wilson's political thought first began to show signs of changing about 1907. By 1910, even before he entered politics, he was a moderate progressive who affirmed that reform of many aspects of American life was overdue. The first sign of this metamorphosis was a significant shift in his thinking about the role that Christians and the church should play in the world at large. He delivered three major addresses on this subject between 1906 and 1909—"The Minister and the Community," in 1906, and "The Present Task of the Ministry" and "The Ministry and the Individual," both in 1909.[15] They revealed that Wilson had not yet altogether shed his earlier pietism and intense individualism. The church's duty, he said, was to save individual souls. Christ was not a social reformer. "Christianity, come what may, must be fundamentally and forever individualistic." The minister should "preach

Christianity to men, not to society. He must preach salvation to the individual." Yet a momentous intellectual ferment was also evidenced in the last two lectures. We find Wilson also saying—not in 1906, but in 1909—that "if men cannot lift their fellow-men in the process of saving themselves, I do not see that it is very important that they should save themselves. . . . Christianity came into the world to save the world as well as to save individual men, and individual men can afford in conscience to be saved only as part of the process by which the world itself is regenerated" and

It seems singular that each generation should ask itself for what purpose the gospel has come into the world, and yet it is necessary, if we would understand our own purposes, that we should ask ourselves in our own generation that fundamental question. No doubt Christianity came into the world to save the world. We are privileged to live in the midst of many manifestations of the great service that Christianity does to society, to the world that now is. . . . In our own day in particular there are a great many notable movements afoot which are manifestly touched—at their root, at any rate—with the spirit of Christ.

Wilson's movement into the ranks of advanced reform after he entered politics is well known. From the beginning of his political career he was in the forefront of the fight to overhaul the political institutional structure. During the first two or three years of his presidency he also fought for and obtained fundamental changes in national economic policies. But he was notably reluctant before 1916 to support or even countenance what might be called advanced social reform, that is, legislation for the protection and welfare of disadvantaged groups, when such legislation involved the direct intervention of the Federal Government in economic and social life.

Wilson crossed his political Rubicon dramatically in 1916 by espousing and winning adoption of a series of measures, including the first Federal child labor law, that put the government, for the first time, squarely into the business of social reform and amelioration. Moreover, he went on during the campaign of 1916 to describe his vision of the new good society in which government would be ceaselessly at work to restrain exploiters, uplift the downtrodden, protect children, and defend the helpless and weak. It was nothing less than a vision of the modern welfare state. Again, the significant fact about his vision was its origin, at least in part, in Wilson's Christian social conscience. Over and over during the campaign he said that Americans had no choice but to carry their compassion and concern into all the byways of life. As he put it in an address at Buffalo on November 1:

There are a great many social questions now with which legislation has to deal, very profound and radical questions. There are questions of justice, there are questions even of moral health. . . . I tell you, my fellow-citizens, until a political party or any other group of men get that thought at their hearts they are unfit for the national confidence. . . . We hold our Christianity as a private, individual matter, if we think of it at all. Our idea is that we will save ourselves, whereas, in my conception, Christianity was just as much intended to save society as to save the individual, and there is a sense in which it is more important that it should save society.[16]

These convictions grew as the years passed. The last words that Wilson published—an article, "The Road Away from Revolution," which appeared in *Atlantic Monthly* in 1923—were a warning to Americans then reveling in materialism that their society could not survive the onslaught of the disinherited unless it became "permeated with the spirit of Christ and . . . [was] made free and happy by the practices which spring out of that spirit." This meant, he made clear, a social and economic order based on "sympathy and helpfulness and a willingness to forego self-interest in order to promote the welfare, happiness, and contentment of others and of the community as a whole. This is what our age is blindly feeling after in its reaction against what it deems the too great selfishness of the capitalistic system."

VI. AMERICA'S MISSION TO THE WORLD
AS MINISTRY

Woodrow Wilson's whole thinking about foreign policy for the United States was shaped by his concept of ministry and his belief in divine providence. Ministry, as he said many times, is Christ's ministry of unselfish service to individuals, societies, and nations. He believed that God had created the United States out of divers people for a specific, almost eschatalogical, role in history—as one scholar has written, "to realize an ideal of liberty, provide a model of democracy, vindicate moral principles, give examples of action and ideals of government and righteousness to an interdependent world, uphold the rights of man, work for humanity and the happiness of men everywhere, lead the thinking of the world, promote peace,—in sum, to serve mankind and progress."[17] Foreign policy should not be used for material aggrandizement, not even defined in terms of material interest. America's mission in the world was not to attain wealth and power, but to fulfill God's plan by unselfish service to mankind.[18]

It is no coincidence that this sounded like the language of the American missionary movements of that day. Wilson believed intensely in an evangelical, missionary church. At Princeton he participated in the World Student Christian movement of the Y.M.C.A. and knew and greatly admired its leader, John R. Mott. It was, he said to the Pittsburgh Y.M.C.A., "an association meant to put its shoulders under the world and lift it, . . . that other men may know that there are those who care for them, who would go into places of difficulty and danger to rescue them, who regard themselves as their brother's keeper." Speaking to the Presbytery of Potomac in 1915 about Christian missions in China, Wilson said:

Why, this is the most amazing and inspiring vision that could be offered to you, this vision of that great sleeping nation suddenly cried awake by the voice of Christ. Could there be anything more tremendous than that? . . . China is at present inchoate; as a nation it is a congeries of parts, in each of which there is energy but as yet unbound in any essential and active unity. Just as soon as its unity comes, its power will come in the world. Should we not see that the parts are fructified by the teachings of Christ?[19]

Wilson came to the presidency, as has often been observed, with no training and little interest in foreign affairs and diplomacy. As President he, of course, had to deal with international problems, and to deal with them immediately in Mexico, the Caribbean area, and the Far East. He simply adopted all his assumptions about the nature of the church's worldwide ministry as the basic assumptions of his foreign policy. And during the first two years of his presidency, he and his Secretary of State, William Jennings Bryan, another Presbyterian elder who shared Wilson's motivation, put into force what has elsewhere been called "missionary diplomacy"[20] aimed at helping underdeveloped countries work toward domestic peace and democracy.

Wilson soon discovered that a diplomacy of helpfulness was immensely difficult, troublesome, and even dangerous. He soon learned that it was not always possible to impose even altruistic solutions on other countries. Experience rapidly dispelled Wilson's naïveté. The hopeful diplomatist became the Christian realist, doing what he could in the consciousness that ideal solutions were not always possible. But Wilson's basic views and motivation never changed. He struggled to avoid involvement in the First World War in part because he ardently desired to use American power for a noble mission—mediation of the conflict. He accepted belligerency in 1917 in large part because he then believed that American participation was now the surest if not the only way to peace. He created the League of Nations in part because he thought that it would be the instrumentality of America's redemptive work in the world. And he spent his health and strength in order to convince Americans that God had laid the burdens of leadership for peace on them. As he said when he presented the Versailles Treaty to the Senate on July 10, 1919: "The stage is set, the destiny disclosed. It has come about by no plan of our conceiving, but by the hand of God who led us into this way. We cannot turn back. We can only go forward, with lifted eyes and freshened spirit, to follow the vision. It was of this that we dreamed at our birth. America shall in truth show the way. The light streams upon the path ahead, and nowhere else."[21]

Another salient aspect of Wilson's fundamental thinking about international relations was an obvious product of his life and faith as a Christian. It was his abhorrence of war as an instrument of national policy. I do not believe that Wilson subscribed to the classical Christian doctrine of the just war, although it must be admitted that we have scanty evidence of his views on this matter. He certainly thought that aggressive war was organized murder, and he burned with shame at the thought that his own country had engaged in aggressive war against Mexico in 1846-1848. But Wilson was not a Christian pacifist. He thought that there were times and places when Christians had to accept war as the less evil option. But when he was forced to lead his country into battle in 1917, he tried to turn evil into good by giving moral purpose to American participation.

This paper has explored Woodrow Wilson's Christian faith and attempted to demonstrate that it was the source and motivation of all his thinking about ethics, political and social action, and America's role in the world at large. It has also tried to show that Wilson was not primarily a moralist, but rather, a Christian realist who lived from day to day by the light that he believed God had given him.

It would now surely be rhetorical to ask whether being a Christian, one profoundly influenced by the Calvinist tradition, made any difference in his life. The record and peculiar character of his contributions to American political traditions gives eloquent answer to this question.[22]

Chapter 10
Our Calvinist Heritage
in Church and State
By George L. Hunt

At the end of his essay on John Calvin in this book, Prof. John T. McNeill observes "there has been in this century no adequate attempt on the part of the churches to confront the nations and the world with a Christian political philosophy." It is not the aim of this series of essays to develop such a philosophy; but it may be possible to indicate how the highway of history—specifically, the history of the Calvinist tradition in Europe and the United States on this subject—can aid in formulating one. It will be the purpose of this concluding chapter to see what each of the persons and periods discussed in this book may contribute to such a philosophy.

We begin, naturally, with the compendium of insights admirably brought together by Professor McNeill in his chapter on Calvin.

EUROPE AND SCOTLAND

The twentieth century has no possibility or intention of creating on the North American continent any coalition between church and state comparable to the one that existed in Calvin's Geneva. Our times are rather one of those fluid periods out of which new concepts may arise and new relationships be formed. If we are not to embrace a Machiavellian cynicism in our political attitudes, we must hope that some of the enduring principles of Calvinism will emerge to clarify and influence the new situation.

Perhaps this is the point at which to begin our summary, for Calvin (as McNeill makes clear in Chapter 1) came on the scene as a necessary corrective antidote to the pure secularism of Machiavelli. The civil order is ordained of God. For the Christian, political affairs cannot be divorced from God. Civil government is an *order:* established by God to keep life orderly. Therefore, the civil magistrate is —whether he acknowledges it or not—in the eyes of Christians called to his service by God and is to be obeyed by Christians as a servant of God. On his part, the magistrate is required to conduct himself in such a way that he will receive the support and approbation of Christians (whether he is a Christian or not), and Christians are to seek political office as an opportunity to express their service to God and men.

The best *form* for a civil government, according to Calvin, is a combination of aristocracy and democracy. However, for us (as well as for Calvin) this is not the aristocracy of the landed gentry or of heredity. It is the "aristocracy of excellence" (McNeill, p. 37), whereby a list of the best men for office are selected by their peers and the names submitted to the electorate. All of us are vividly aware of the many factors that play on nominating committees and nominating conventions, so that we will not always accord to such an "aristocracy" the high esteem they may theoretically deserve; yet plain common sense indicates the wisdom of such a procedure. Perhaps a contemporary application of this principle would be greater involvement of high-minded Christian people in political parties and in decision-making at the party level; the independent who eschews such involvement is often left with little or no choice when election time comes.

"Resistance to tyranny" is a third principle suggested to us by our reading of Calvin. Calvin was not a revolutionary ready to incite a riot on the least provocation. Resistance to government was, for him, a last resort, but it was necessary if the magistrates forsook their calling to be obedient to God. It is not necessary to comment on this principle further at this point, since it recurs frequently in the thought and action of the other men we shall be considering.

Dr. McNeill indicates that the kind of relation between church and state known in Calvin's Geneva would be inoperable today (even if it were deemed wise) because of the denominational and religious pluralism on the contemporary scene. It does not follow, of course, that churches should unite today in order to exert stronger, more direct political influence. We do not want either a state church or a church state. But it is this religious diversity which makes our present church-state relationship necessary, and it is our denominational fragmentation that makes the church as ineffective as it is in the political area. This is only to say that the development of a Christian political philosophy, if such a thing is possible, will not be purely Presbyterian or Calvinist and should not be so.

With Philip Mornay we turn to the role of Calvinism in the political ferment of sixteenth-century France.

Civil war in France between Protestants and Catholics began in 1562, two years before Calvin's death, and continued until the Edict of Nantes in 1598. During this time Calvinists vigorously espoused in writing and in action a concept of government that owed its inspiration in large measure to the political thought of Calvin. In the situation that prevailed, however, French Calvinism was not the nonviolent kind; it was led by men of war, men with a passionate desire for freedom, men with a drive to form a new nation. It is worthwhile to repeat Professor Fuhrmann's description of the legacy handed on from Calvin to the Huguenot movement:

What is common to early Calvinism and to the new Huguenot world is that no priest stands between God and man.

The spring of religion is open to all men and women. The faithful now willingly associate in faith, in prayer, in love, and the good life. The minister is no longer a priest but one of the brethren whose assignment is to diffuse the Word of God and to extend charity. Calvin's religion had summed this new lay world without dominating it. Some civic and political liberties were born of this religious liberty. The greatest quality of the Huguenot was indeed the ability to govern himself. And this control of self, this moral sovereignty of the person brought about an entirely new idea and type of individual, social, and political life. We have here, not an equalitarian and flat democracy, but a varied society, hence a colorful society, hence a free society.

Mornay's role in this movement was to be political philosopher, statesman, conciliator between the aggressors of revolution. There is no need to repeat the record of his work as our author has given it to us, but it is important to note what happens when a Calvinist like Mornay seeks to express his faith in action.

Under a consuming conviction of the sovereignty of God, this kind of Calvinist believes that the king rules under the control of God and by the will of the people. He rules, not by his own authority and power, but by virtue of a divine contract or constitution with God, the monarch, and the representatives of the people. When the monarch violates the contract and becomes an idolatrous tyrant, the people can rebel against him.

This kind of Calvinist is not willing to observe a benign neutrality in political matters. He will find the political leader who best embodies the virtues of piety, justice, and charity, and align himself with him.

This kind of Calvinist sees the importance of the separation of political powers for the civil rights and liberties of the people. "I am the law!" is the voice of tyranny, whether in seventeenth-century France or in some local police force in the United States; he who executes the laws cannot also be he who creates them.

Democracy has its roots in such thinking.

When we turn to Samuel Rutherford and the Scottish Reformation, an American Presbyterian feels he is beginning to move into more familiar territory. A firm respect for law and order is coupled with a healthy suspicion of those who seek too much power and authority for themselves, and we find these fundamental attitudes attributable to Scottish heritage as well as to theological principles. Professor Maclear's statement: "Scottish political experience remained predominantly that of a pluralistic society with diffused political power, suspicious of royal centralization, and emotionally committed to the defense of 'true religion' against the political manipulations of the crown" (p. 69) has a distinctly modern application for Americans.

Calvinist theology gave already established political concepts their needed religious purpose and dynamic, so that the struggle for freedom had this new dimension. It also provided support for the rebellion against idolatrous sovereigns and magnified the concept of the covenant beyond its Huguenot application to the point where it became the rallying point for the people in their relations with government.

It is also significant that church-state relations in Scotland led to a polity that

required the eradication of episcopacy and the establishment of ministerial parity and conciliar government, that is, an ecclesiastical establishment practically impossible for the crown to control. It may be less certain, but still possible, that analogically this polity also suggested the value of mixed aristocracy and democracy operating under law. But most importantly, Presbyterian partisans adopted the two kingdom theory of church-state relations, already formulated in the Second Book of Discipline, by which clerical claims for the independence of the church were significantly broadened. Where Scottish Reformers, following conventional Reformation practice, had sought the rule of godly government (though locating this corporately in the Estates rather than in the crown), Melville and his followers argued for the church's perfect freedom in her own spiritual realm where the magistrate, however bound by responsibilities to the church, possessed no authority or right distinct from that of other Christians. While this doctrine also taught the Christian magistrate's freedom from clerical dictation, its practical effect in Scotland was to promote the exclusion of the king as king from ecclesiastical decision.

In *Lex rex*, Rutherford developed the doctrine of the covenant in such a way as to allow the now-familiar resistance to authorities who break it. But the tone of his disputation is remarkably egalitarian and "extreme" (Maclear). What sounds new to us is his great faith in "the people." We are moving away from the aristocracy of Geneva and France; this quotation bears repeating:

The people have a naturall throne of policie in their conscience to give warning, and materially sentence against the King as a Tyrant. . . . Where Tyranny is more obscure, . . . the King keepeth possession; but I deny that Tyranny can be obscure long.

The main theme of *Lex rex*, says Professor Maclear, is the authority of law:

All rightful authority lies in law, whether it is authority of king, estates, populace, or kirk. The king is truly king only when he identifies himself with the law, and only to the degree that he succeeds in voicing and implementing law.

When a particular religious faith is so closely tied with the destinies of a nation as was Presbyterianism in Scotland, there is bound to be the intolerance and the religious nationalism that our author has indicated (pp. 81-82). Since this same spirit will reappear in New England Calvinism, we may wonder if intolerance and religious nationalism are indigenous to Calvinism. Perhaps we may say they grow out of it naturally, but are not its best fruits or its inevitable consequences.

Rutherford teaches us respect for the law, respect for the people, the freedom of the church from the state, a wise recognition of the limits placed on human institutions (even church councils), and the duty of sovereigns to rule as under God, bound in covenant with him and with the people.

FROM THE PURITANS TO WOODROW WILSON

With Ahlstrom's essay on Puritanism in America we cross the ocean and devote ourselves from this section on to Calvinism on this continent.

Professor Ahlstrom deals almost entirely with the effect of Puritanism upon "the moral attitudes of the people toward governmental functions, governors and judges, law and order, civic duties and rights" (p. 97). He does not describe for us the Holy Commonwealth of New England in which state and church were closely knit. In his judgment this relationship is not the contribution of New England Calvinism to American political thought that we should stress. Rather, he would have us see the *sense of civic responsibility* as the gift of Calvinism or Puritanism to the present day.

The Puritan faith had within it a "peculiar power to mold personal values, to gird the citizen or magistrate for his work, to arouse and maintain his sense of civic duty, to intensify his determination to live responsibly before and under the law, and to make him aware that neither individual men, or groups of men, or even nations, were above the law or were laws unto themselves" (p. 98). Respect for law, which we saw in Rutherford, is one of the foundations of this faith. It was based upon the "conviction that the Bible, through command, counsel, and historical example, provided precise divine guidance for church, state, and personal life" (p. 101). Moreover, the law was not simply binding upon the Christian in his individual and personal affairs. After the pattern of Israel in the Old Testament, God's law was the law of the people, the corporate nation. It is easy to see the Calvinism in this emphasis.

The sense of divine call, which so deeply informs the Puritan ethic and classical American democracy, is also a Calvinistic legacy; we shall see it illustrated in Abraham Lincoln. This commitment to a vocation "provided a kind of inner, subjective support to faithful and serious performance of these worldly callings—whether they be in the family, the marketplace, or in the state" (p. 104). Perhaps it would be too much to claim that residual Calvinism in our democracy accounts for the deep sense of responsibility to the common weal held by statesmen today; men have many different motivations to such service. Yet the fact that this thread of Puritanism has been woven into our national ethos is at least good reason for the modern heirs of Calvin to keep the spirit strong.

An intense respect for law leads easily into legalism and moralism, those whipping boys of contemporary ethical theory. The "bluenose" and the legalist are perversions of the Calvinistic spirit. Yet respect for law and a development of a fresh, creative attitude toward standards and authority is one of the desperate needs of our relativistic, somewhat amoral age. Can we refocus law within the context of grace, as the Reformers tried to do? This would seem to be one of the tasks to which the modern heirs of Calvin and Luther might be called. The contribution of this venture to a "Christian political philosophy" would be invaluable.

One reason for the essay on Locke in this volume is to provide the bridge between New England Calvinism and the work of Witherspoon and his heirs. The "bridge" is by way of Locke and Roger Williams, the "heretic" so far as many New England Calvinists were concerned and the hero so far as the free church tradition in America is concerned.

Are we claiming more for Calvinism than we should as we seek to embrace Locke and Williams into its fold? Professor Hudson (a Baptist) thinks not. He believes that

these men ought to be placed in the line of Calvin via the
Independent movement in England. Calvin's political
theory is broad enough to encompass both the Holy Commonwealth of New England and its "rebel" of Rhode
Island, for at its heart Calvinism is more a matter of
certain principles than of a particular structural, political
application.

Hudson's three Locke-Williams principles are clearly
stated, although the second one—segregation—has a much
different meaning today than it did in colonial minds, and
we might wish we could use another word. The three
principles are: fallibility, segregation, and consent.

Fallibility led to freedom from enforced religious conformity and this became the watchword of the English
Independents. Yet its roots lie in the Reformation and
its application is seen in the Presbyterianism both of
Rutherford and Witherspoon, who made much of the
fallibility of church councils.

Segregation implied the separation of church and state
that we have also seen in Rutherford and will see in
Witherspoon. But it is important to underline the fact that
this was not withdrawal of the church from the world, as
the principle might be applied by some pietistic sects.
Rather, the implication of the principle is that, although
no particular church may ask for special privilege and
protection from the state, church and state are both under
the surveillance and sovereignty of God. "The two realms
of nature and grace were equally under the government
of God" (p. 127). Professor Hudson has pointed to the
confusion and ambiguities involved in an application of
this principle; it is worth noting that there is still a great
deal of confusion in the application of the same principle
today.

The principle of consent means that since the church is
a voluntary society, no one can come into it by coercion
but only by his own consent. One must have freedom of
conscience in his religion. We may seem to be far from

some applications of Calvinism here; and yet is this not inherent in the Reformation rediscovery of the freedom of the Christian man? At any rate, American Calvinism, from Witherspoon on, insists on this freedom, and its source is Calvinistic at least to this extent that it comes through the Locke-Williams line of Reformation thought.

Before we turn to John Witherspoon it may be wise to recognize the shift in political thought in general that began with the eighteenth century. Locke and Williams are precursors of this shift to some extent. John Wise (early eighteenth century) is one of its eloquent spokesmen. But we need to understand what happened if we are to see Witherspoon in perspective.

Perry Miller's introduction to the section on "The Theory of the State and of Society" in the collection of readings entitled *The Puritans* summarizes the matter for us:

In the eighteenth century, "for the first time since the fall of the Roman Empire religion could be separated from politics, doctrinal orthodoxy divorced from loyalty to the state, and the citizens of a nation permitted to worship in diverse churches and to believe different creeds without endangering the public peace. Various factors contributed to effecting this revolution; the triumph of scientific method and of rationalism made impossible the older belief that government was of divine origin; the rise of capitalism, of the middle class, and eventually of democracy necessitated new conceptions of the role of the state. Social leadership in England and America was assumed by a group of gentlemen who were, by and large, deists or skeptics, and to them all religious issues had become supremely boring. At the same time the churches themselves, particularly the newer evangelical denominations, were swinging round to a theology that made religious belief the subjective experience of individual men, entirely unrelated to any particular political philosophy or social theory."[1]

This shift would have been incomprehensible to the early seventeenth-century Puritans. In their age "the unity of religion and politics was so axiomatic that very few men would even have grasped the idea that church and state could be distinct. For the Puritan mind it was not possible to segregate a man's spiritual life from his communal life."[2]

If there is to be the "Christian political philosophy" of which we spoke at the beginning of this essay, it will certainly have to come to grips with the shift Miller has described and consider how the church today is relating to the political order and how it should do so. Obviously we cannot return to the "Holy Commonwealth" of Puritan New England, even if we desired to do so; yet are we simply to follow the individualistic line of evangelicalism? The rediscovery of the corporateness of the church, which has taken place in our century, leads us to feel that mere individual influence is not enough. But what is the answer? And does Calvinism, as we are examining it, give us clues toward the answer?

Professor Nichols' essay on John Witherspoon may provide us with one such clue as he discusses the meaning of the ambiguous principle called "the separation of church and state." In terms of the Preliminary Principles to the Presbyterian Form of Government as well as the First Amendment to the Constitution of the United States the principle is related more to religious liberty than it is to an impregnable "wall" between the two orders. What we have here, firmly endorsed by the American Presbyterian Church of the colonial period and held ever since, is the principle of religious tolerance, derived through the Separatist–Locke–Williams tradition of Calvinism rather than through the Winthrop line.

This is clear enough so far as tolerance is concerned. The colonial Presbyterian stand on the obligations of the state to the church is less clear, as Professor Nichols points out. The state "was not expected to be neutral as between the religious and the unreligious" (p. 138). It might even, in Witherspoon's mind, support religion financially, provided it did this with full recognition of the rights of dissenters. The concluding quotation in Nichols' essay, from a contemporary source, indicates, as we are all well aware, that the meaning of "separation" is still not settled.

Every church would like to claim Abraham Lincoln, the statesman who joined no church. On what basis do we include him in this book on Calvinism and the political order? Professor Wolf gives ample testimony to the presence of Calvinistic ideas in Lincoln's thought and their direct affect upon his actions. The themes are so clearly stated at the end of Wolf's essay that they do not need to be repeated here.

What we have in Abraham Lincoln is a President for whom the absolute separation of the state from religious motivations and concerns is unthinkable. So far as he is concerned, this is a nation under God, and the American people have a destiny given by God to be a people mindful of his will and committed to his service. They are God's "almost chosen people." Lincoln would have been the last person to foster intolerance or to establish a denominationally inspired theocracy (i.e., a state church); but this does not prevent him from believing that we are a religious people and are, as a nation, instruments in the hand of God for the doing of the divine will. Furthermore, the God he worships and sees guiding us is the Christian God, the God of the Bible. He is not nebulous about his faith.

The role of the church in the Civil War reflects a situation that Elwyn Allen Smith has described as follows:

The outbreak of slavery controversy after 1830 dealt a paralyzing blow to Calvinist concern for public affairs. Southern Presbyterians insisted that slavery was a political, not a moral, question. Northerners saw that if slavery dispute should ever intrude on the churches, they would be divided. There was wide agreement both north and south that the debate on slavery should be separated from religion. Even this point of view commanded no consensus, however, and division descended relentlessly on the American churches.

Partly because so many churches split over politics, by 1840 the notion that a line should be drawn between all public affairs and spiritual religion was widespread among American Christians. A mood of withdrawal was in the air. Where Presbyterians had once worked in legislatures and executive offices to change the country, they now retired to their closets for prayer.[3]

We may infer from this statement that the church did not officially seek to influence public policy on the issues of slavery or the Civil War, although we may be sure individual churchmen on each side of the conflict were hardly neutral. Lincoln, therefore, stands as an individual Christian, aided by the preaching he had heard and the reading he had done, but expressing in word and action one man's sense of duty in doing the will of God.

However, Smith goes on to point out that after 1870 a new climate began to be felt in the churches.

The era of withdrawal did not end quickly—many members of large modern denominations still consider religion a purely private matter—but the wind changed about 1870. Shortly after the end of the Civil War, industrial development spurted forward, particularly in the northeastern quarter of the nation. Its side effects shocked and aroused the Christian conscience. Slums and poverty had always existed in the cities of America, but now the swift expansion of industry created great concentrations of workers around factories. Newly arrived immigrants, often disoriented, were at the mercy of unemployment and corrupt political machines.

North America was founded by immigrants, but the arrival of massive minority groups that knew nothing of the Puritan tradition was another matter. The Irish, solidly Roman Catholic, came by the hundred thousands after 1830 and settled in urban ghettos. The slaves had followed a religion of mixed paganism and lay Christianity but until their emancipation were looked on rather as property than persons. After their liberation they began to move to the cities.

Between 1890 and 1920, when immigration was drastically curbed, the industrial cities of the nation received wave upon wave of peoples who erected their own churches, founded their own social clubs, and often lived cheek by jowl. By 1870, the country was no longer Protestant; by 1910, the hinge of its economic life was the factory, not the farm.

Just as 1770 marked the beginning of a new century in the political life of our country, 1870 opened a new chapter in the social awareness of the American churches. Within forty years all the major churches of the country had recognized that the mood of withdrawal was unfit for the new times. Separation of church and state was indispensable, but the continued isolation of the churches from the lives of people struggling for existence in industrial society would be fatal to religion.

Christians pondered what they should do. Should churches speak out about child labor? Should they do something about drunkenness? Political corruption? Strikes? Were these any concern of churches as such?

While considerable numbers still doubted whether religion belonged in factories, saloons, and legislative halls, a significant clerical leadership answered these questions with an unmistakable Yes. But how the churches should act was not so clear. Was the church going to intervene in affairs of state?

For many centuries, churches had relieved human misery by acts of charity. The baffling new feature of the industrial age was that charity could not rebuild cities, annul obsolete laws, or regulate labor practices. These goals could be achieved only by new legislation. Should church influence be brought to bear on lawmaking? Would this breach the precious wall separating church and state? If the church should advocate relief of social suffering by law, could this be done without infringing church-state separation?

By 1910 the leading American churches were reasonably sure that it was morally obligatory for them to seek justice for workers who could not obtain a fair share of the product of their labor. Churchmen knew that this must be accomplished bv law. They affirmed that there must be no mixing of institutional church power with government power but demanded strong representations of Christian opinion by churchmen and others of similar views to legislators and public executives. American Protestant leadership was once again taking responsibility for the whole life of the society.[4]

Was this climate influential on Woodrow Wilson, the last of the "Calvinists" to be studied in this book and the

statesman for whom this lectureship is named? Wilson
was a son of the Presbyterian manse, deeply imbued in
Presbyterian ethos and theology. How did his Calvinist
heritage affect his conduct of public office?

Arthur Link demonstrates clearly the answer to both
questions. It is fascinating to note Wilson's shift from a
laissez-faire individualist to a strong believer in the role
of the state in social reform. The shift parallels exactly
what Smith has described in the quotation given above.
One might question Professor Link's statement that
scholastic Presbyterianism can be characterized as
"pietism, individualism, and almost total rejection of
organized social action either by religious or political
communities" (p. 167). The story we have traced in
this book would suggest at least that there is nothing
"un-Presbyterian" or "un-Calvinistic" about corporate social involvement. The reader is referred to the description
of Calvinism quoted at the beginning of Wolf's essay on
Lincoln (p. 140) to support the view that as Wilson turned
to social reform with missionary zeal, he was exemplifying
Calvinism at its best.

WHAT HAVE WE LEARNED?

Our survey is now complete so far as the chapters in
this book are concerned. But when a study of Calvinism
in the twentieth century is made it will have to take into
account man and movements of our time that are too
immediate for us to evaluate. For example, the resurgent
Calvinism of Karl Barth and the influential ethical thinking of the Niebuhrs—both products of the Reformed tradition—will occupy a significant place in such a study.
The role of the Confessing Church under Hitler[5] and the
reaction of contemporary theologians to communism[6] will
also be data for this historian. It is, of course, notably
true that theological thought today has crossed over denominational and traditional lines, so that the Calvinist
tradition has rightly been fused with many others. No one
is going to argue that the "Christian political philosophy"

that may be developed should be Calvinist, Lutheran, or Free Church. It will probably be all three—and more! But what if Calvinism should be embodied in such a philosophy? In other words, what in Calvinism is of lasting value and speaks to us today, specifically in the area of political affairs?

Our study seems to me to have brought these principles of a developing Calvinism to the forefront:

1. The civil order is ordained of God. Whether it comes out of God's special revelation in the Bible or through his activities in the mind and reason of men, it is still of God and is under his authority. We have seen that although Biblical religion is absolutely formative and definitive for the Calvinist, he can also recognize that God works outside the Bible as well as in it and through it.

2. Calvinism moved from the "aristocracy" attitude toward a confidence in the good sense and wisdom of the common people. (Rutherford; Lincoln.)

3. The Christian may resist tyrants and a tyrannical government, but should do so cautiously and only as a last resort.

4. Calvinists will be in the forefront of every drive for liberty and freedom. (Mornay; Rutherford; Witherspoon; Lincoln; Wilson.)

5. The concept of compact or covenant is at the heart of Calvinist political theory. We have seen that the concept can be variously interpreted and applied; but basically it means that the governor rules by the consent of the governed and in a pact expressing mutual responsibility. Both are under God. The foundation of this principle in the Bible is obvious, as is its commonplace existence in democracy. But it was by no means obvious or commonplace when first formulated and later forged out on the anvil of history!

6. A corollary to the covenant idea is the teaching that the king must rule under law and under the authority of his legislators and advisers. Respect for law and order,

so marked in Rutherford and the Scottish Revolution, is singled out by Ahlstrom as an important element in our Puritan legacy.

7. Human institutions, including church councils, do err, and fallible men need checks and balances on their leaders and institutions.

8. Men are called into service of church and nation by the voice of God and are to rule in godly fear and faithfulness to his example of justice, charity, and compassion.

9. Calvinism developed a tolerance for dissenters and nonbelievers that is not antithetical to its theology but which awaited the Independent movement in England and the Presbyterian movement in America for its expression. This principle became imbedded in later Calvinism.

10. The state must allow complete religious freedom to the church. (Witherspoon.)

11. Separation of church and state does not necessarily imply that a nation must divorce itself completely from a religious consciousness or from religious impulses. Lincoln's sense of "this Nation under God" has somehow to be understood a) in relation to a definite awareness of God which will not b) impose itself upon those who do not have the same definiteness or awareness. Tolerance within conviction: how can it be achieved?[7]

12. A nation and church with a sense of mission will adapt itself to changing times and changing needs. (Wilson.)

"Should the church get into politics?" is the question we hear frequently asked. For Calvinists the question is only a little over a hundred years old, and is an American question, not a Calvinist one! *How* the church or the Christian does this is a debatable matter; but *that* they should be involved in the struggles of men to provide a life "with liberty and justice for all" is not even debatable for those who are in the heritage of John Calvin.

Notes

CHAPTER 1. CALVINISM AND EUROPEAN POLITICS IN HISTORICAL PERSPECTIVE (McNEILL)

1. G. H. Williams, *The Norman Anonymous of 1100 A.D.* (Harvard University Press, 1951).

2. It is impossible to indicate in what degree Calvin in his religious outlook was indebted to Luther, Bucer, Melanchthon, Zwingli, and other Protestant predecessors.

3. Q. Breen, *John Calvin: A Study in French Humanism* (Wm. B. Eerdmans Publishing Company, 1931), p. 80.

4. W. S. Hudson, *John Ponet (1516?–1556), Advocate of Limited Monarchy* (The University of Chicago Press, 1942). It contains a facsimile reproduction of *A Shorte Treatise of Politike Power.*

5. John Knox, *History of the Reformation in Scotland,* ed. by W. C. Dickinson (Thomas Nelson & Sons, 1949), II, pp. 129–130.

6. Buchanan's work, *The Powers of the Crown in Scotland,* is translated by C. F. Arrowhead (University of Texas Press, 1949).

7. For a penetrating discussion of the treatises of Hotman and Bodin, see B. Reynolds, *Proponents of Limited Monarchy in Sixteenth Century France* (Columbia University Press, 1931).

8. P. S. Gerbrandy, *National and International Stability: Althusius, Grotius, Van Vollenhoven* (Harvard University Press, 1944), p. 13.

9. For interpretation and bibliography of Jurieu, see G. H. Dodge, *The Political Theory of the Huguenots of the Dispersion with Special Reference to the Thought and Influence of Pierre Jurieu* (Columbia University Press, 1947).

10. R. F. Harvey, *Jean Jacques Burlamaqui: A Liberal Introduction to American Constitutionalism* (The University of
North Carolina Press, 1937).

CHAPTER 2. JOHN CALVIN ON CIVIL GOVERNMENT (McNEILL)

1. Dates of the letters are given for the convenience of those
who may wish to verify the passages.

2. *Geneva and the Coming of the Wars of Religion in
France, 1555–1563* (Geneva: E. Droz, 1956), p. 43.

3. *L'Action politique de Calvin hors de Genève* (Geneva:
Georg, 1909), pp. 11 ff.

4. Pierre Janelle, discussing the angry conference in which
Gardiner confronted Bucer and Alexander Alesius over this
issue, thinks Calvin may have been present in it. *Obedience in
Church and State* (Cambridge: University Press, 1930), p. xliv,
note 4.

5. *La Conjuration d'Amboise et Genève* (Geneva, 1922),
pp. 46 f.

6. In a study stressing the influence of Bucer upon Calvin's
political ideas, H. Baron thinks Calvin's term *"magistratus
populares"* is a modification of Bucer's *"magistratus inferiores,"
Church History,* VIII (March, 1939), p. 38. Cf. M.-E. Chenevière, *La Pensée politique de Calvin* (Geneva: Éditions Labor
et Fides, 1937), pp. 341 f.

7. Commentary on *De Clementia,* v. 54; v. 6.

8. *Institutio principis Christiani,* 1516.

9. See J. Pannier, *Recherches sur la formation intellectuelle
de Calvin* (Paris: Alcan, 1931), pp. 12–27; Q. Breen, *John
Calvin: A Study in French Humanism* (Wm. B. Eerdmans
Publishing Company, 1931), pp. 77–85, 113 ff., 121 ff., 145.

10. *Les Origines de la Réforme* (Paris: Hachette, 1935), IV.
p. 15.

11. English text from *Calvin: Theological Treatises,* ed. and
tr. by J. K. S. Reid (The Library of Christian Classics, Vol.
XXII; The Westminster Press, 1954), pp. 32 f.

12. Text in P. Barth and Wilhelm Niesel, *Johannis Calvini
opera selecta* (Munich: Kaiser, 1936), Vol. I, pp. 416 f., by
P. T. Fuhrmann, *Calvin: Instruction in Faith* (The Westminster Press, 1949), pp. 76 ff.

13. One of three Biblical texts that find mention in the
Seneca Commentary, a work not Biblically oriented.

14. *Calvin's Doctrine of the Christian Life* (Edinburgh and London: Oliver and Boyd, Ltd., 1959), Part III, Ch. v.

15. *The Theology of Calvin*, tr. by H. Knight (London: Lutterworth Press, 1956), p. 230.

16. Cicero, *De legibus*, III. i. 2.

17. *Institutes*, IV. xx. 9–11.

18. *Institutes*, IV. xx. 14, 16.

19. John Knox, in a letter to Mrs. Anna Locke, 9th December, 1556, *Works of John Knox*, ed. by D. Laing, IV, 240.

20. Commentary on I Cor., ch. 5. Cf. *Institutes*, II. xv. 3–5, on Christ's kingly office.

21. Cf. J. T. McNeill, "Natural Law in the Teaching of the Reformers," *Journal of Religion*, XXVI (1946), pp. 168–182.

22. *L'Humanisme social de Calvin* (Geneva: Éditions Labor et Fides, 1961), p. 29. This book is available in English as *The Social Humanism of Calvin*, tr. by Paul T. Fuhrmann (John Knox Press, 1964). In *Institutes*, IV. xx. 24–25, Calvin states very strongly the duty of obedience even where the magistrates show "no appearance of the image of God."

23. *Institutes*, IV. xx. 8.

24. *Institutes*, IV. xx. 8.

25. Zwingli, *Exposition of the Christian Faith*, in *Zwingli and Bullinger*, tr. by G. W. Bromiley (The Library of Christian Classics, Vol. XXIV; The Westminster Press, 1953), p. 266.

26. The French edition of 1543 reads somewhat differently at this point: "*Vrai est que si on fait comparaison des trois espèces de gouvernement que j'ai récitées, que la prééminence de ceux qui gouverneront tenant le peuple en liberté sera plus à priser.*"

27. *Republic*, VIII. ii.

28. *Politics*, IV. vi. 3.

29. For Calvin's part in this revision, see M.-E. Chenevière, pp. 205–224.

30. *Institutes*, IV. xx. 8.

31. Commentary on Micah 5:5 (1560).

32. See note 6.

33. Professor Chenevière, stressing Calvin's "perhaps," calls in question the common assumption that he here intends an allusion to the constitutional function of the French Estates General. Yet the same author presents evidence that about 1560–1562 Calvin was counting upon the Estates General to relieve persecution in France (Chenevière, pp. 335, 344 ff.). In 1536, when Calvin wrote this, the Estates, which at one time had challenged the royal prerogative, had not been called

for thirty years, and it was not until the year following the
1559 edition that the body was assembled. But Calvin knew its
historical role, and his "perhaps," insofar as it applied to
France, may have been inserted wistfully.

34. Passages from *Institutes,* IV. xx. 29–30, have been utilized.

35. *Calvini opera, Corpus Reformatorum* edition, XLI, 25.

36. See my note in The Library of Christian Classics edition
of Calvin's *Institutes* (Vol. XXI; The Westminster Press, 1960),
p. 1518, note 54.

37. Letter to Viret, October, 1542.

Chapter 3. Philip Mornay and the Huguenot Challenge to Absolutism (Fuhrmann)

1. PRIMARY SOURCE:

*Mémoires et Correspondance de Duplessis-Mornay . . . édition
complète . . . précédée des Mémoires de Madame de Mornay
sur la vie de son mari* (Paris: Treuttel et Würtz, 1824–1825),
12 vols. (Mornay).

GENERAL HISTORIES:

Jacques Ellul, *Histoire des institutions,* II (Paris: P.U.F., 1956)
(*HI*); Paul T. Fuhrmann, *An Introduction to the Great
Creeds of the Church* (The Westminster Press, 1960); John T.
McNeill, *The History and Character of Calvinism* (Oxford
University Press, 1957); Jean Touchard, *Histoire des idées
politiques,* I (Paris: P.U.F., 1959). The part referred to was
written by Pierre Jeannin (*HIP*).

MONOGRAPHS ON THIS PERIOD:

John T. McNeill, *Unitive Protestantism—A Study in Our Religious Resources* (Abingdon Press, 1930); Paul F.-M. Méaly,
*Les Publicistes de la Réforme sous François II et Charles IX—
Origines des idées politiques libérales en France* (Paris: Librairie Fischbacher, 1903) (Méaly); Giuliano Procacci, *Classi
sociali e monarchia assoluta nella Francia della prima metà
del secolo XVI* (Turin: G. Einaudi, 1955).

MONOGRAPHS ON MORNAY:

Joachim Ambert, *Duplessis Mornay ou Études historiques et
politiques sur la situation de la France de 1549 à 1623,* 2d ed.
(Paris: Comptoir des Imprimeurs-Unis, Comon et Cie., 1848);
Henri Duval, *Éloge de Duplessis-Mornay—Discours* (Paris:

F. Buisson Libraire, 1809) (Duval); Raoul Patry, *Philippe Du Plessis-Mornay—Un Huguenot homme d'État* (Paris: Librairie Fischbacher, 1933) (Patry). Reviewed by John T. McNeill in *Journal of Religion,* XIII (1933), pp. 338–339.

2. Méaly, p. 257.

3. Méaly, pp. 147–148.

4. Méaly, p. 218.

5. P. Jeannin in J. Touchard, *HIP,* I, pp. 278–282.

6. Boxed statement in E. Jarry, *Les Temps modernes* (Paris: Les Éditions de l'École, ca. 1959), p. 101.

7. In Méaly, p. 17.

8. Such German horsemen were (and are) called *reîtres* in French. To this day, *reître* stands for a coarse, greedy, and cruel man.

9. In Germain Martin, *Les Grands Messieurs qui firent la France* (Paris: J. Gibert, 1945), p. 20.

10. G. Martin, p. 20.

11. This great king was unfortunately assassinated in 1610. We had then a new queen, a new king. In 1624, Cardinal Richelieu became premier, carrying on the program of abasing the political power of the Huguenots and making the king truly absolute. We all know how King Louis XIV later repealed the Edict of Nantes (1685), and many Huguenots had to leave France, go to Germany and England. Their contribution helped to make these nations great industrial powers.

12. M.-J. Gaufrès in Lichtenberger, ed., *Encyclopédie des sciences religieuses* (Paris: Fischbacher, 1880), IX, p. 426 (*ESR*).

13. In Patry, p. 19.

14. Mornay, I, p. 45; Patry, p. 24.

15. Mornay, I, p. 72.

16. Patry, pp. 272, 274.

17. It was republished with a substantial introduction by H. J. Laski, *A Defense of Liberty Against Tyrants* (London, 1924).

18. Such as J. Ellul, *HI,* II, p. 278.

19. Such as Méaly, p. 222, and C. Petino in *Enciclopedia Cattolica* (Vatican City, 1950), IV, pp. 1995–1996.

20. In Méaly, pp. 222–223.

21. Mornay, I, p. 81. Mme Mornay's life of her husband can be read in English under this title: *A Huguenot Family in the XVI Century—The Memoirs of Philip de Mornay Written by His Wife,* tr. by Lucy Crump, with an Introduction (London: George Routledge & Sons, n.d.).

22. G. T. van Ysselsteyn, Patry, and P. Jeannin, *HIP*, I, p. 278.

23. In *Revue historique*, May, 1931.

24. (1) Must subjects *obey* a prince when his orders are contrary to the will of God? Answer: Kingship presupposes a contract between God and king and a contract between king and people. The orders of a prince ought not to be preferred to God's will. Duties to God come first.

(2) Is it legitimate to *resist* a prince who violates God's law and ruins the church? Answer: When the prince ruins religion, he ought to be resisted. Magistrates have control over the prince. Private men ought to offer a passive resistance until magistrates call them to arms.

(3) Does the same apply to purely *secular interests?* Answer: Men have established kingship for security abroad and at home. Kings ought to enforce the law. A first kind of tyrants are usurpers. These are outlaws; any citizen can kill them. A second kind of tyrants are legitimate kings who neglect their duties. Officers and nobles ought to lead them back to duty even by force. This is the reason why officers and magistrates exist. Their destroying tyranny serves the state.

(4) Ought *neighboring* princes help those who are afflicted for cause of religion or oppressed by tyrants? Answer: There is only one church whose head is Jesus Christ. If a member is stricken, all others ought to help him. As for civic affairs, charity ought to move a prince to defend the oppressed and force tyrants back to reason. (Patry, p. 277.)

25. Whether the two friends cooperated beforehand, each furnishing materials that Mornay put together, or whether Mornay simply added of his own to a manuscript furnished by Languet, our two historians would not decide for lack of data. (Patry, pp. 277–278.)

26. J. Ellul, *HI*, II, pp. 278–279.

27. In Lichtenberger, ed., *ESR*, VII, p. 73.

28. *The New Schaff-Herzog Encyclopedia of Religious Knowledge* gives it as translated into English (*Discourse of Life and Death*) by Edward Aggas (London, 1577, and six later editions).

29. Mornay, I, p. 119.

30. This work was translated and published in English in 1579, 1581, and 1606.

31. Patry, pp. 52–53.

32. Mornay, I, p. 129.

33. Translated and published in English as *A Worke Concerning the Trewness of the Christian Religion* (1587; 4th ed., 1617).

34. Patry, pp. 293, 300.

35. Mornay, II, pp. 189–193. Advice given to the King of Navarre, Jan. 9, 1583.

36. Mornay, II, p. 394, Dec. 18, 1583, to Montaigne.

37. *Ibid.*, p. 401, last day of 1583, to Montaigne.

38. Mornay, II, pp. 380–393, April 24, 1484.

39. John T. McNeill, *Unitive Protestantism*, p. 269.

40. *Lacrimae*, tr. by G. J. Healed (London, 1609). Two other works of Mornay were put into English: *The Institution, Usage and Doctrine of the Holy Sacrament* (London, 1600) and *The Mysteries of Iniquitie that is Historie of the Papacie*, tr. by S. Lennard (London, 1612).

41. In Patry, p. 611.

42. Méaly, p. 246.

43. In Patry, p. 617.

44. In Duval, p. 14.

45. In Patry, p. 618.

46. Patry, p. 618.

47. Méaly, p. 246.

48. Méaly, p. 252.

49. Duval, p. 39.

CHAPTER 4. SAMUEL RUTHERFORD: THE LAW AND THE KING (MACLEAR)

1. A brief sketch of Rutherford's life is in *Dictionary of National Biography*, ed. by Leslie Stephen and Sidney Lee (London: Oxford University Press, 1921–1922) (*DNB*). Several uncritical accounts exist, but there is no adequate modern life.

2. *Letters of Samuel Rutherford*, ed. by Andrew Alexander Bonar (Edinburgh: W. P. Kennedy, 1863), I, p. 163.

3. For the Aberdeen situation and tradition, see David Mathew, *Scotland Under Charles I* (London: Eyre & Spottiswoode, Ltd., 1955), pp. 80–91; and especially W. G. Sinclair Snow, *The Times, Life, and Thought of Patrick Forbes, Bishop of Aberdeen, 1618–1635* (London: S.P.C.K., 1952).

4. *The Letters and Journals of Robert Baillie*, ed. by David Laing (Edinburgh: R. Ogle, 1841), I, pp. 8–9. *Peaceable and Temperate Plea* answered the claims of independency.

5. Bonar, II, p. 314. Dated May 25, 1644.

6. In addition to *Lex rex: The Due Right of Presbyteries* (London, 1644); *The Tryal & Triumph of Faith* (London, 1645); *The Divine Right of Church-Government* (London, 1646); and *Christ Dying and Drawing Sinners to Himself* (London, 1647). The works against sects and toleration, *A Survey of the Spirituall Antichrist* (London, 1648) and *A Free Disputation against Pretended Liberty of Conscience* (London, 1649), may have been composed in England.

7. Bonar, II, p. 365. Dated May, 1651.

8. *Lex rex* in its English setting is discussed by most histories of English political thought. See, for example, G. P. Gooch, *The History of English Democratic Ideas in the Seventeenth Century* (Cambridge University Press, 1898), pp. 115–116, and Perez Zagorin, *A History of Political Thought in the English Revolution* (London: Routledge & Kegan Paul, Ltd., 1954), pp. 5–6. For the place of *Lex rex* in contract theory, see J. W. Gough, *The Social Contract* (Oxford: Clarendon Press, 1957), pp. 93–94. J. W. Allen, *English Political Thought 1603–1660* (London: Methuen & Co., Ltd., 1938), pp. 285–288, gives little attention to Rutherford's publications and stresses the piety evident in his letters.

9. On this subject, James Mackinnon, *The Constitutional History of Scotland* (London: Longmans, Green & Co., 1924), is useful. The pluralism of Scottish society was more complicated than indicated here. Town councils and conventions of royal burghs had important administrative and fiscal powers.

10. Examples of sixteenth-century bands of manrent and friendship will be found in *A Source Book of Scottish History*, ed. by William Croft Dickinson and Gordon Donaldson (London: Thomas Nelson & Sons, 1954), III, pp. 389–394.

11. Major lectured to both Knox and Buchanan. For brief estimates of Major in relation to Scotland, see J. W. Allen, *A History of Political Thought in the Sixteenth Century* (London: Methuen & Co., Ltd., 1928), pp. 336–337, and Mackinnon, p. 190.

12. Quoted in J. H. M. Salmon, *The French Religious Wars in English Political Thought* (Oxford: Clarendon Press, 1959), p. 91. Estimate of Buchanan in Allen, *History of Political Thought in the Sixteenth Century*, pp. 336–342.

13. John Neville Figgis, *Political Thought from Gerson to Grotius, 1414–1625* (Harper & Row, Publishers, Inc., 1960), pp. 151–152.

14. See account in Allen, *History of Political Thought in the Sixteenth Century*, pp. 106–116.

15. Robert Bruce and Robert Rollock, both of Edinburgh, seem to have been the earliest preachers of covenant doctrine. Rutherford himself produced *The Covenant of Life* (Edinburgh, 1655). The development of the political use of the covenant is described in S. A. Burrell, "The Covenant Idea as a Revolutionary Symbol: Scotland, 1596–1637," *Church History*, X, No. 4 (Dec., 1958), pp. 338–350. I am indebted to this article for several useful suggestions.

16. John Row, *The History of the Kirk of Scotland from the Year 1558 to August 1637* (Edinburgh: Maitland Club, 1842), p. 239.

17. Gordon Donaldson, *The Scottish Reformation* (Cambridge: University Press, 1960), pp. 183-202. The English story is told in A. F. Scott Pearson, *Church and State* (Cambridge: University Press, 1928).

18. Donaldson, pp. 130 ff. The quotation is from *The Autobiography and Diary of Mr. James Melville*, ed. by Robert Pitcairn (Edinburgh: Wodrow Society, 1842), p. 370.

19. For interpretation of the revolt, see Mathew, pp. 243–305. For the king's own interpretation, see *A Large Declaration Concerning the Late Tumults in Scotland* (1639). There is evidence that by 1640 the combination was breaking apart, with moderates and peers opposing Argyll and the kirk (see Mathew, pp. 291 ff.). Wide subscription had been solicited for earlier covenants, but not on a comparable scale. Yet not many signatures were secured in Aberdeen or the Highlands.

20. Bonar, II, pp. 31, 214–215, 171–172.

21. Ablest of the bishops, Maxwell took a leading part in the development of the Scottish Prayer Book of 1637. As an energetic and ambitious executive, he threatened the nobles. Mathew, p. 250, quotes Bishop Guthry: "Now among these late bishops whom King Charles preferred none were generally esteemed gifted for the office except Bishop Maxwell, of whom it cannot be denied, that he was a man of great parts; but the mischief was, they were accompanied with unbounded ambition, for it did not content him to be a lord of the secret Council (as were the rest) but he behoved also to be a lord of the exchequer, and a lord of session extraordinary, and at last to be lord high treasurer, which proved fatal to them all." See sketch in *DNB*. Maxwell's thought is placed in context in Salmon, pp. 91–92.

22. *Lex rex* also appeared in an Edinburgh edition in 1644. Subsequently, it appeared as *The Preeminence of the Election of Kings* (London, 1648); *A Treatise of Civil Policy* (London, 1657); and with its original title in 1686.

23. *Lex rex: The Law and the Prince. A Dispute for the Just Prerogative of King and People. Containing the Reasons and Causes of the Most Necessary Defensive Wars of the Kingdom of Scotland, and of their Expedition for the Ayd and Help of their Dear Brethren of England* (London, 1644), p. 9. Rutherford deals with these royalist arguments in Questions XII and XIII. See also pp. 448–449. In arguing the conquest question, Rutherford treats the case of King Fergus, not that of William the Conqueror.

24. *Lex rex*, pp. 101–102.

25. *Ibid.*, pp. 96 ff. Charles II heard Rutherford deal with the subject personally: "He past to St. Andrews; where at the Entry Mr. Rotherford Head of one of the Colledges made Him an Oration; and amongst other His Expressions told Him, that if He persisted not in the Covenant *Actum est de Rege, & Re Regia*" (Sir Edward Walker, *Historical Discourses upon Several Occasions* [London, 1705], p. 160).

26. *Lex rex*, p. 106: "But the generall covenant of nature is presupposed in making a King, where there is no vocall or written covenant, if there be no conditions betwixt a Christian King and his people, then those things which are just and right according to the law of God and the rule of God in moulding the first King, are understood to regulate both King and People, as if they had been written: and here we produce our written covenant, Deut. 17. 15. Josh. 1. 8. 9. 2 Chr. 31. 32."

27. *Ibid.*, pp. 250–251. For Rutherford's explicit justification of the Tables, see p. 464.

28. *Ibid.*, pp. 58, 159–176, 405.

29. *Ibid.*, pp. 389, 441. Note also pp. 12–13: "Reformation of Religion is a personal act that belongest to all, even to any one private person according to his place."

30. *Ibid.*, pp. 103, 113–114. James had himself used this royalist argument in *The Trew Law of Free Monarchy* (1598).

31. *Ibid.*, p. 399.

32. *Ibid.*, p. 184.

33. *Ibid.*, p. 434.

34. *Ibid.*, pp. 81–82.

35. Bonar, II, p. 409.

36. *Survey of Spirituall Antichrist*, Part II, pp. 99–100; *Lex rex*, p. 428.

37. *Free Disputation*, pp. 46, 51, 52, 54, 185–188. *Survey of Spirituall Antichrist*, p. 261.

38. *Survey of Spirituall Antichrist*, p. 333. *Due Right of Presbyteries*, p. 394.

39. *Free Disputation*, pp. 177–182.

40. Note the statement in "Epistle," *Due Right of Presbyteries:* "In God's matters there be not as in grammar the positive and comparative degrees; there are not here truth and more true and most true. Truth is an indivisible line which hath no latitude and cannot admit of splitting."

41. *Free Disputation*, p. 360.

42. *A Testimony to the Truth of Jesus Christ* (Edinburgh, 1703), pp. 4–5. Dated Oct., 1658. A newsletter from Scotland indicates English reaction to Rutherford's activity, January, 1651, when Rutherford and others protested to Lambert: "You will perceive by itt the drift of their intencions, which is to exalt their Governement into their owne handes *in ordine ad spiritualia*, to vilifie the proceedings of the Parliament of the Commonwealth of England, and scandalize the practice of the officers of the Army in their most religious performances, and to perswade both to lett them have a liberty to tyrannize both over the bodies and soules of the poore people under pretence of giving them liberty of conscience, which cannott stand with the principles of any who are lovers of true freedome either to their outward or inward man" (C. H. Firth, *Scotland and the Commonwealth* [Edinburgh: T. and A. Constable, 1895], p. 33).

43. Thomas Aikenhead was executed for blasphemy in 1696. A Toleration Act was passed by the British Parliament in 1712, largely for the benefit of Episcopalian Dissenters. Penal laws, kept alive partly by Jacobite alarms, were not repealed until the end of the eighteenth century.

44. Bonar, II, pp. 253–254, 256.

45. Rutherford is preoccupied with this theme throughout his correspondence. See, for example, Bonar, II, pp. 160, 162, 197, 256, 269, 336, 341, 353, 354–355, 361, 365, 394. See also the conclusion of Samuel Rutherford, *A Sermon Preached to the Honorable House of Commons: At their Late Solemne Fast, Wednesday, Janu. 31 1643* (London, 1644), p. 64.

46. [David Calderwood] *The Speach of the Kirk of Scotland to Her Beloved Children* (1620), pp. 5–6. Compare also G. Gillespie, *A Dispute against the English-Popish Ceremonies* (1637), p. 3: "The Church of Scotland was blessed with a more glorious and perfect Reformation, than any of our neighbour Churches." Note Rutherford's letter in 1651, after refusing an offer from Utrecht, to dissuade a correspondent from leaving Scotland: "I see it, and find it, that the Lord hath covered the whole land in a cloud in His anger. But though

I have been tempted to the life, I had rather be in Scotland beside angry Jesus Christ, knowing that He mindeth no evil to us, than in any Eden or garden in the earth; if we can remain united with the Lord's remnant in the land" (Bonar, II, p. 369). Yet Rutherford made clear to English critics that the faith he served was not a national faith. See *Peaceable and Temperate Plea,* Introduction, p. 2.

47. Burrell, p. 348. See also Bonar, I, p. 111; II, pp. 142–143.

48. Bonar, I, p. 111: *Quaint Sermons of Samuel Rutherford* (London: Hodder & Stoughton, 1885), p. 36. The same hopes were publicly announced in "To the Reader," *Peaceable and Temperate Plea,* p. 3.

49. Bonar, II, pp. 171–172 (dated Sept. 10, 1637); II, p. 378.

50. *Ibid.,* pp. 419–420.

51. See especially *An Apologeticall Relation, of the Particular Sufferings of the Faithfull Ministers & Professors of the Church of Scotland Since August, 1660* (1665); *Naphtali* (1667); [Sir James Steuart] *Jus Populi Vindicatum* (1669). *The Apologeticall Relation* suggests the eventual passing of the reaction but regrets that it will arise from political rather than religious demands. "May not the peers & body of the Land come at length to supplicate his majesty, to loose this yoke from off their necks, when their Scottish . . . spirits shall not be able any longer to endure such unsufferable slavery: This is not impossible, nay nor improbable: Though it were to be wished, That they might Act that way, upon some other principles, principles of piety & godly tendernesse; That, seeing their injury done to Christ, in shaking off his government & lawes, . . . they might lament after the Lord, & seek him with the whole heart, & engadge themselves in a Covenant with the Lord, to be for him to the utmost of their power, & bring the land back againe to seek the Lord God of their fathers." ("Epistle," p. 25.)

52. Cameronian declarations and the Claim of Right are given in Dickinson and Donaldson, III, pp. 174–184, 200–207.

53. Steuart became Scottish Lord Advocate after the Revolution. See article in *DNB.*

54. See William Haller, *Liberty and Reformation in the Puritan Revolution* (Columbia University Press, 1955), pp. 8, 104 ff.

55. See Richard Schlatter, *Richard Baxter and Puritan Politics* (Rutgers University Press, 1957).

56. I have not found reference to *Lex rex* in eighteenth-century Scottish political writers. Dugald Stewart in his *Prog-*

ress of Metaphysical, Ethical and Political Philosophy said
that of previous writers, Buchanan was most congenial to the
age. See Caroline Robbins, *The Eighteenth-century Common-
wealthman* (Harvard University Press, 1959), p. 179. Several
contemporary opinions of Rutherford may be cited. Gooch,
p. 115, quotes Bishop Guthry: "Everyone had in his hand
Rutherford's new book, *Lex rex,* stuffed with questions that in
the time of peace would have been judged damnable treason,
but were now so idolised that whereas in the beginning
Buchanan was looked on as an oracle, he was now slighted as
not antimonarchical enough." *The Historical Works of Sir
James Balfour* (Edinburgh: W. Aitchison, 1824–1825), III,
p. 413: "Mr. Samuell Rutherfurd, altho lousse in hes youthe,
hes beine from his first begining a suorne enimey to mon-
archey, as hes writtings testifie; a hatter of all men not of hes
oppinion, and one quho if neuer so lightlie offendit, vnrecon-
cilable; woyd of mercey and charity, altho a teacher of both
to others." The date was 1649. Lastly, Charles II's Lord Advocate, Sir George Mackenzie, linked *Lex rex* in 1684 with
Buchanan, *Naphtali,* and *Jus populi vindicatum* as "Ring-
leaders, who have endeavoured extreamly to poyson this Nation by perswading the People" to treasonable political doctrine (Sir George Mackenzie, *Jus regium: Or, the Just and
Solid Foundations of Monarchy in General; And More Especially of the Monarchy of Scotland* [London, 1684], p. 4).

57. Peter Heylyn in his *History of Presbyterianism* said that
every true Scot accepted the sovereignty of the people and the
right of deposition (cited in Gooch, p. 114). For an example
of popular appropriation of covenant political theory, see *An
Humble Remonstrance of the Citizens of Edenburgh to the
Convention of the Estates of Scotland Concerning the Kings
Majestie and the Kingdome of England with a Declaration
Touching the Covenant of the Kingdomes, and Propositions for
Peace* (1648).

58. *Lex rex,* Preface, pp. 2, 1.

CHAPTER 5. THE PURITAN ETHIC AND THE SPIRIT OF AMERICAN
DEMOCRACY (AHLSTROM)

1. This paper was presented in the Woodrow Wilson Lec-
tureship of the National Presbyterian Center at the First
Presbyterian Church, Stamford, Conn., on Jan. 19, 1964. In
May, 1962, its author had delivered the Third Hooker Lecture

at the First Church of Christ, Hartford, Conn., on the subject "Thomas Hooker, Puritanism, and Democratic Citizenship: A Preliminary Inquiry into Some Relationships of Religion and American Civic Responsibility." That lecture was privately published by the First Church, and in slightly revised form it appeared in *Church History*, XXXII, Dec., 1963. Its chief purpose was to move the discussion of Hooker and democracy toward a more general consideration of early New England Puritanism as a whole. Since both that essay and this one deal with essentially the same problem, several elements of the earlier argument are repeated. It is the author's intention, however, that this essay should complement the Hooker study.

2. Charles H. and Katharine George, *The Protestant Mind of English Reformation* (Princeton University Press, 1961).

3. "A Modell of Christian Charity," in *The Puritans*, 2 vols., ed. by Perry Miller and T. H. Johnson (Harper Torchbook, 1963), I, p. 199.

4. *War and the Intellectuals*, ed. by Carl Resek (Harper Torchbook, 1964), pp. 156–161; Van Wyck Brooks, *The Wine of the Puritans* (1909); Howard A. Bridgman, *New England in the Life of the World* (The Pilgrim Press, 1920), pp. 4–5; H. H. Saunderson, *Puritan Principles and American Ideals* (The Pilgrim Press, 1930).

5. Edward S. Morgan, *The Puritan Dilemma* (Little, Brown and Company, 1958); Ola Winslow, *Master Roger Williams* (The Macmillan Company, 1957); Perry Miller, *Roger Williams* (The Bobbs-Merrill Company, Inc., 1953); Mauro Calamandrei, "Neglected Aspects of Roger Williams' Thought," *Church History*, XXI (Sept., 1952); Le Roy Moore, "Roger Williams and the Historians," *Church History*, XXXII (Dec., 1963); the historical works cited in my essay on Hooker, and in Winthrop S. Hudson's essay in this volume.

6. See George A. Cook, *John Wise, Early American Democrat* (Columbia University Press, 1952).

7. Dissents were entered by various Baptist, Anglican, and Quaker historians, for example, Isaac Backus, *History of New England* (1777–1796), and Samuel A. Peters, *General History of Connecticut* (1781), but these did not turn the tide. See also Carl Bridenbaugh, *Mitre and Scepter* (Oxford University Press, Inc., 1962).

8. Lyman Beecher, "The Memory of Our Fathers," *Works*, 3 vols. (Boston, 1862), I, pp. 315–343; "The Republican Elements of the Old Testament," I, pp. 175–190; "The Bible a Code of Laws," II, pp. 154–203.

9. George Bancroft, *History of the United States,* rev. ed., 6 vols. (Boston, 1876); especially his summary estimate, I, pp. 369–377. John Gorham Palfrey, *History of New England,* 5 vols. (Boston, 1858–1890). Neither of these magisterial historians must be sold short, however. Their respective achievements have never been equaled.

10. Williston Walker, *Creeds and Platforms of Congregationalism* (The Pilgrim Press, 1960), Ch. 18.

11. See Frank Hugh Foster, *The Modern Movement in American Theology* (Fleming H. Revell Company, 1939).

12. See, for example, Herbert Baxter Adams, *The Germanic Origin of New England Towns* (Johns Hopkins University, 1882).

13. See Bernard Bailyn's recent survey of literature and posing of the problem: "Political Experience and Enlightenment Ideas in Eighteenth-Century America," *American Historical Review,* LXVII (Jan., 1962), pp. 229–251.

14. See my "Continental Influence on American Christian Thought since World War I," *Church History,* XXVII (Sept., 1958) and "Theology and the Present-Day Revival," *Annals,* Vol. 332 (Nov., 1960), reprinted in *Not Many Wise* (The Pilgrim Press, 1962).

15. Miller's corpus includes many essays and books on other related topics: the movement from "Edwards to Emerson," Transcendentalism and its leading writers, and the continuing impact of Puritanism. In regard to the topic at hand, see especially, "From Covenant to Revival," in *The Shaping of American Religion,* ed. by J. W. Smith and A. L. Jamison (Princeton University Press, 1961). No American historian of the twentieth century has done so much to make the mind and literature of Puritanism an object of serious attention among interpreters and historians of the American experience.

16. "The Social Context of the Covenant," *Bulletin of the Congregational Library,* VI (Jan., 1955), pp. 17–19.

17. Brooks Adams, *The Emancipation of Massachusetts* (1887). See also James Truslow Adams' three-volume history of New England, especially the first volume: *The Founding of New England* (Little, Brown and Company, 1921, 1949; recently reissued).

18. See note 5 above.

19. See Herbert Butterfield, *The Whig Interpretation of History* (London, 1931).

20. Max Weber, *The Protestant Ethic and the Spirit of Capitalism,* first published in 1904–1905. Talcott Parsons'

translation, published in 1930, is now available in a Scribner's paperbound edition. (Close attention to Weber's extensive annotation is imperative. R. H. Tawney's introduction to the translation is misleading.) *Protestantism and Capitalism: The Weber Thesis and Its Critics*, ed. by Robert W. Green (D. C. Heath and Company, 1959), samples the ensuing controversy and provides a bibliography. See also Reinhard Bendix, *Max Weber* (Oxford University Press, 1946; reissued by Doubleday Anchor Books), and H. Stuart Hughes, *Consciousness and Society* (Alfred A. Knopf, Inc., 1958). Ralph Barton Perry's *Puritanism and Democracy* (The Vanguard Press, Inc., 1944) is the most valuable American study of the civic implications of Puritanism. Its argument is implicitly Weberian. More directly apropos is Karl H. Hertz, "Max Weber and American Puritanism," *Journal for the Scientific Study of Religion*, I (Spring, 1962), pp. 189–197. See also in the same issue (pp. 226–227) Talcott Parsons' review of one of the more recent and more unfortunate forays into this realm: Kurt Samuelsson, *Religion and Economic Action* (Basic Books, Inc., Publishers, 1961; also in Harper Torchbook edition).

21. One very succinct statement of the purpose of founding Holy Commonwealths in New England was given by Governor Winthrop while he was yet on board the *Arbella* in 1630: "The end is to improue our liues to doe more seruice to the Lord, the comforte and encrease of the body of christe whereof wee are members, that our selues and posterity may be the better preserued for the Common currupcions of this euill world, to serue the Lord and worke out our Salvacion vnder the power and purity of his holy Ordinances. . . . That which the most of theire Churches maineteine as a truthe in profession onely, wee must bring into familiar and constant practice." ("Modell of Christian Charity," in Miller and Johnson, eds., *The Puritans*, I, pp. 197–198).

22. Francis Grund, *Aristocracy in America* (Harper Torchbook, 1959), pp. 212–213.

23. Grund, "The Americans in Their Moral, Social and Political Relations," from the selection in Henry S. Commager, ed., *America in Perspective* (The New American Library of World Literature, Inc., 1948), p. 75.

24. Alexis de Tocqueville, *Democracy in America*, 2 vols., ed. by Phillips Bradley (Alfred A. Knopf, Inc., 1946), I, pp. 247–248.

25. James Bryce, *The American Commonwealth*, 3 vols.

(London: The Macmillan Company, 1888), III, pp. 340, 352. See Ch. xcvi, *passim*.

26. D. W. Brogan, *The American Character* (Alfred A. Knopf, Inc., 1944, 1956), pp. 17–19.

27. This is not to say that Americans have any guarantee as to the permanence of this legacy. Indeed, the frequent reference to the present as a time of "post-Protestant" pluralism may betoken the beginning of the end of the "Puritan era" in American history; and this fact is probably not unrelated to the moral consternation of our times.

28. This legalistic precisionism is put in sharp relief by Horton Davies, *The Worship of the English Puritans* (London: The Dacre Press, 1948).

29. See the discussion of this issue in Perry Miller, *Roger Williams*, and Calamandri, *loc. cit.* (note 5 above).

30. Miller and Johnson, eds., *The Puritans*, I, pp. 209–210.

31. Connecticut Historical Society *Collections* (Hartford, 1860), I, pp. 20, 21; quoted and discussed in George Leon Walker, *Thomas Hooker, Preacher, Founder, Democrat* (New York, 1891), p. 125.

32. Miller and Johnson, eds., *The Puritans*, I, pp. 206–207.

33. John Cotton stated the heart of the matter straightforwardly: "We live by faith in our vocations, in that faith, *in serving God, serves men, and in serving men, serves God: . . .* so that this is the work of every Christian man in his calling, even then when he serves man, he serves the Lord; he doth the work set before him, and he doth it *sincerely,* and *faithfully*" (Miller and Johnson, eds., *The Puritans*, I, p. 322).

34. See note 20 above.

35. *The Excellency of a Publick Spirit* (Boston, 1702), pp. 24, 25.

36. See Bendix, pp. 49 ff., 269 ff.

37. "Antinomianism" generally refers to views that are in some sense "against" the "law" (*nomos*); more precisely, the view that under the gospel dispensation the moral law is of no use or obligation, faith or the work of the Spirit being alone necessary for salvation. Rarely did it imply libertinism. "Nomianism" is simply a name coined to designate the opposite view, i.e., legalism.

38. The Anne Hutchinson affair was indeed a crisis and an extraordinarily revealing one, especially for the theme of this essay. We should ask, What would have been the civic legacy of a Holy Commonwealth presided over by Mistress Anne? See three recent studies and the older and newer literature

that they cite: Edmund S. Morgan, *The Puritan Dilemma* (Little, Brown and Company, 1958); Larzer Ziff, *The Career of John Cotton* (Princeton University Press, 1962); and Emery J. Battis, *Saints and Sectaries* (The University of North Carolina Press, 1962).

39. Franklin's prudential counsels are, if anything, too well-known; that they represent a secularized form of the "Puritan ethic," however, can hardly be denied. Needing emphasis in the present context is the civic dedication exhibited by his entire career. See *Benjamin Franklin and the American Character*, ed. by Charles L. Sanford (D. C. Heath and Company, 1955), representative critical essays and bibliography.

40. George Wilson Pierson, "The Obstinate Concept of New England: A Study in Denudation," *New England Quarterly*, XXVIII (March, 1955), pp. 16–17.

41. The manner, meaning, and implications of this evangelical blending of Puritan and Enlightened ideas is in actuality "the great problematic in the interpretation of *ante-bellum* Protestantism," a subject to which I recur in a forthcoming essay. The literature is vast, but see Ralph Henry Gabriel, *The Course of American Democratic Thought* (The Ronald Press Company, 1940, rev. ed., 1956), Chs. ii and iii. See also note 8 above.

42. Grund, "The Americans," as given in Commager, ed., *America in Perspective*, p. 73.

CHAPTER 6. JOHN LOCKE: HEIR OF PURITAN POLITICAL
THEORISTS (HUDSON)

1. Herbert D. Foster *Collected Papers* (privately printed, 1929), p. 151.

2. Edmund Burke, *On Conciliation with the American Colonies, Works of Edmund Burke* (London: Henry G. Bohn, 1856), I, 466; see also *Puritanism and Liberty*, ed. and with an Introduction by A. S. P. Woodhouse (London: J. M. Dent & Sons, Ltd., Publishers, 1939), p. 70. *The Works of John Adams*, ed. by C. F. Adams (Little, Brown and Company, 1850–1856), VI, p. 4.

3. See cartoon reproduced as frontispiece in Carl Bridenbaugh, *Mitre and Sceptre*, where crowd is pictured hurling copies of Locke, Sidney's *Government*, and Calvin's *Works* in their successful effort to prevent the landing of a bishop in America.

4. Whereas Hooker, for example, thought of the church as the nation in its religious aspect, Locke insisted that the church could be no more than a voluntary group within the nation. Furthermore, whereas a key point in Hooker's argument was his insistence that the magistrate could legislate concerning matters "indifferent," Locke insisted that the magistrate had no authority in such matters.

5. Woodhouse, pp. 39, 57–60.

6. Du Moulin was described by Anthony Wood as "a fiery, violent, and hotheaded Independent." H. R. Fox Bourne, *The Life of John Locke* (London, 1876), I, p. 55.

7. Bagshaw was not a radical. He affirmed the authority of the monarch in the life of the church so long as it was "in the Lord." But he did insist that the magistrate may not impose things indifferent and that efforts to suppress heresy are unprofitable and often dangerous. "As winds till they are pent up and restrained from their motion do seldom haunt, so nor heresies neither till they are imposed and forced they make no public disturbance." His work was issued in three parts: *The Great Question Concerning Things Indifferent* (London, 1660); *The Second Part of the Great Question* (London, 1661); *The Necessity and Use of Heresies, or The Third and Last Part of the Great Question* (London, 1662).

8. Maurice Cranston, *John Locke: A Biography* (The Macmillan Company, 1957), p. 60.

9. *Ibid.*, p. 82.

10. The essay is printed in H. R. Fox Bourne, I, pp. 174–194.

11. For a discussion of the Calvinism of Arminius, see Foster, p. 142.

12. The best statement of this four-point argument is *An Apologetical Narration* (London, 1643) issued by the Dissenting Brethren of the Westminster Assembly. It is reprinted in William Haller, *Tracts on Liberty in the Puritan Revolution*, (Columbia University Press, 1934), pp. 307–339. Evidence of this point of view appears repeatedly in the writings of the early New Englanders; see W. S. Hudson, "Denominationalism as a Basis for Ecumenicity," *Church History* (March, 1955), pp. 32–50.

13. John Cook, *What the Independents Would Have* (London, 1647), p. 12. Jeremiah Burroughes, *Irenicum* (London, 1646), pp. 92, 207, 242–245; Woodhouse, p. 259.

14. Reprinted in Woodhouse, pp. 247–248.

15. *Ibid.*, pp. 300, 301.

16. Speech III in *Oliver Cromwell's Letters and Speeches*,

ed. by Thomas Carlyle (Wiley and Putnam, 1871), IV, p. 61.
And Cromwell added: "This, I say, is a Fundamental." *Ibid.*,
p. 62.

17. Woodhouse, p. 226.

18. John Locke, *Four Letters on Toleration* (London:
Ward, Locke and Co., Ltd. n.d.), p. 5.

19. *Ibid.*, pp. 7–10, 13, 18, 32.

20. *The Complete Writings of Roger Williams,* ed. with an
Essay by Perry Miller, 7 vols. (Russell & Russell, Inc., Publishers, 1963), III, pp. 160–162, 228, 354.

21. *Ibid.*, III, pp. 333, 73, 258, 395, 335, 201, 392; VI, p. 347.

22. *Ibid.*, IV, p. 251. For Williams, "civil justice" was the
equivalent of "natural right." The meaning is precisely the
same.

23. *Ibid.*, III, pp. 372–373.

24. Locke, pp. 14–15, 6.

25. Williams, III, pp. 232, 252–254.

26. Locke, p. 22.

27. *Ibid.*, p. 27.

28. *Ibid.*, pp. 26, 27, 30–31, 34, 35, 7.

29. Williams, VII, pp. 179–180. See also III, pp. 230–231,
387–388. Locke, p. 24.

30. Williams, III, p. 252.

31. Woodhouse, pp. 250–251.

32. Williams, III, pp. 3–4, 206, 322, 373. See also III, 374–
375.

33. Locke, pp. 4, 36, 37. See also pp. 32–33.

34. Williams, III, p. 193; IV, p. 358.

35. Locke, pp. 2, 4, 26.

36. *Ibid.*, p. 25.

37. Williams, III, 232, 355, 398–399.

38. Locke uses religion to mean that which has to do with
salvation. This is confusing because God is not excluded from
the natural order. Williams occasionally slips into this usage,
but more generally he uses "spiritual" or "soul causes" when
referring to matters that relate to salvation.

39. Williams gives the conventional explanation that had
been elaborated by many Calvinist political theorists with regard to government having its origin in both God and the
people. The magistrate is a minister of God, for "magistracy
in general is of God for the preservation of mankind in civil
order and peace," but "magistracy in special . . . is of man"
(Williams, III, p. 398). Thus "every lawful magistrate . . .
is not only the minister of God but the minister or servant of

the people also [who set up a particular form of government and choose him] . . . , and that minister or magistrate goes beyond his commission who intermeddles with that which cannot be given him in commission from the people" (*ibid.*, IV, p. 187). A magistrate "can have no more power than fundamentally lies in the bodies or fountains [the people], which power, might, or authority is not religious, Christian, etc., but natural, human, and civil" (*ibid.*, III, p. 398). This restriction is implicit in the whole theory, for "a civil government is an ordinance of God" for this purpose, "to conserve the civil peace of people so far as concerns their bodies and goods" (*ibid.*, III, p. 249).

40. *Ibid.*, III, p. 399.

41. Sidney E. Mead, *The Lively Experiment* (Harper & Row, Publishers, Inc., 1963), p. 35. See also pp. 38–54.

CHAPTER 7. JOHN WITHERSPOON ON CHURCH AND STATE (NICHOLS)

1. W. Sargent, *Loyalist Poetry of the Revolution* (Philadelphia, 1857), I, pp. 9–12.

2. John Witherspoon, *Lectures on Moral Philosophy*, Collins ed. (Princeton University Press, 1912), pp. 70, 71, 111.

3. J. T. McNeill, "Natural Law in the Teaching of the Reformers," *Journal of Religion*, XXVI (1946), pp. 168, 182.

4. Ch. 23, iii.

5. *Records of the Presbyterian Church*, 1729, pp. 94 f.

6. Witherspoon, pp. 111–113.

7. As Mr. Pfeiffer has argued in *Religion in America*, ed. by J. Cogley (Meridian Books, Inc., 1958), p. 60.

8. In Cogley, *op. cit.*, pp. 96 f., 115.

CHAPTER 8. ABRAHAM LINCOLN AND CALVINISM (WOLF)

1. John T. McNeill, *The History and Character of Calvinism* (Oxford University Press, 1954), p. 436.

2. Edmund Wilson, *Eight Essays* (Doubleday & Company, Inc., 1954), p. 189.

3. Benjamin P. Thomas, *Lincoln's New Salem*, rev. ed. (Alfred A. Knopf, Inc., 1954), p. 89.

4. Statement of December 24, 1872, quoted in William Barton, *The Soul of Abraham Lincoln* (George Doran Co., 1920),

p. 164. See also William Wolf, *The Religion of Abraham Lincoln* (The Seabury Press, Inc., 1963), p. 86.

5. *The Collected Works of Abraham Lincoln*, ed. by Roy P. Basler (Rutgers University Press, 1953) (henceforth CWAL) I, p. 382.

6. *CWAL*, V, pp. 103–104.

7. *CWAL*, IV, p. 236.

8. *CWAL*, IV, pp. 220–221.

9. *CWAL*, IV, p. 270.

10. James Nichols, *Democracy and the Churches* (The Westminster Press, 1951), p. 270.

11. *Atlantic Monthly* (March, 1909), p. 369.

12. *CWAL*, V, p. 420.

13. *CWAL*, III, pp. 204–205.

14. *CWAL*, IV, p. 274.

15. F. Carpenter, *Six Months with Lincoln at the White House* (Century House Americana, 1961), p. 282.

16. *CWAL*, IV, p. 482.

17. *CWAL*, VIII, pp. 55–56.

18. *CWAL*, VII, p. 542.

19. *CWAL*, VIII, p. 356.

20. *CWAL*, VIII, p. 403.

21. *CWAL*, VIII, p. 399.

22. *CWAL*, VII, p. 302.

23. J. Porter and W. Wolf, *Toward the Recovery of Unity: The Thought of F. D. Maurice* (The Seabury Press, Inc., 1964), pp. 222–223.

CHAPTER 9. WOODROW WILSON: PRESBYTERIAN IN GOVERNMENT (LINK)

1. Speech at Mansion House, London, Dec. 28, 1918, *The Public Papers of Woodrow Wilson, War and Peace*, ed. by Ray S. Baker and William E. Dodd, 2 vols. (New York, 1927), I, p. 346; hereinafter cited as *War and Peace*.

2. Mrs. Crawford H. Toy, "Second Visit to the White House," diary entry dated Jan. 3, 1915 (MS. in the Ray Stannard Baker Collection of Wilsonia, Library of Congress).

3. The foregoing is a brief summary of my "Woodrow Wilson and the Life of Faith," *Presbyterian Life*, XVI (March 1, 1963), pp. 8–12; see also Theodore W. Hunt, "Woodrow Wilson's Attitude Toward Religion" (MS. dated 1924 in the Library of Princeton Theological Seminary).

4. W. Wilson to Ellen A. Wilson, Aug. 10, 1913, Eleanor

W. McAdoo, ed., *The Priceless Gift* (McGraw-Hill Book Company, Inc., 1962), p. 292.

5. W. Wilson to Mary A. Hulbert, Aug. 10, 1913, Ray S. Baker, *Woodrow Wilson: Life and Letters,* 8 vols. (Doubleday & Company, Inc., 1927–1939), IV, pp. 271–272.

6. See James H. Taylor, *Woodrow Wilson in Church* (Charleston, S. C., 1952), for an intimate memoir of Wilson's relations with Central Presbyterian Church, and the letters between President Wilson and Dr. Taylor, now deposited in the Historical Foundation, Montreat, N. C.

7. The following is an incomplete list of these papers and addresses: "Religion and Patriotism," *Northfield* [Mass.] *Echoes,* IX (July, 1902), pp. 217–221; *The Young People and the Church* (Philadelphia, 1905); *The Present Task of the Ministry* (Hartford, Conn., 1909); *The Ministry and the Individual* (Chicago, 1910); "The Bible and Progress," *The Public Papers of Woodrow Wilson, College and State,* ed. by R. S. Baker and W. E. Dodd, 2 vols. (1925), II, pp. 291–302; address to Trenton Sunday school assembly, Oct. 1, 1911, *Trenton True American,* October 2, 1911; *The Minister and the Community* (New York, 1912); "Militant Christianity," address before the Pittsburgh Y.M.C.A., Oct. 24, 1914, *The Public Papers of Woodrow Wilson, The New Democracy,* ed. by R. S. Baker and W. E. Dodd, 2 vols., (1926), I, pp. 199–209, hereinafter cited as *The New Democracy;* address before the Federal Council of the Churches of Christ in America, Dec. 10, 1915, *ibid.,* pp. 429–445; address at his grandfather's church in Carlisle, England, Dec. 29, 1918, *War and Peace,* I, pp. 347–348; "The Road away from Revolution," *ibid.,* II, pp. 536–539.

8. See the notes of chapel talks on April 5, 1891, Nov. 8, 1896, and May 27, 1900, and of talks before the Philadelphian Society, Nov. 2, 1899, and Feb. 20, 1902, all in the MSS. papers of Woodrow Wilson, Library of Congress; baccalaureate addresses delivered on June 12, 1904, and June 11, 1905, *ibid.; The Free Life* (New York, 1908), Wilson's baccalaureate address in 1907; and baccalaureate addresses delivered on June 7, 1908, June 13, 1909, and June 12, 1910, MSS. in the Princeton University Library.

9. *A Many-Colored Toga: The Diary of Henry Fountain Ashurst,* ed. by George F. Sparks (University of Arizona Press, 1962), p. 84.

10. R. S. Baker, memorandum of conversations with Stockton Axson, Feb. 8, 10, and 11, 1925, Baker Collection.

11. C. T. Grayson, *Woodrow Wilson: An Intimate Memoir* (Holt, Rinehart and Winston, Inc., 1960), p. 106.

12. Arthur Walworth, *Woodrow Wilson,* 2 vols. (Longmans, Green & Co., Inc., 1958), II, p. 419.

13. Address before the Pittsburgh Y.M.C.A., Oct. 24, 1914, *The New Democracy,* I, p. 206.

14. H. C. F. Bell, *Woodrow Wilson and the People* (Doubleday & Company, Inc., 1945), p. 379.

15. See n. 7 for bibliographical references. "The Minister and the Community," delivered in 1906, was published in booklet form in 1912.

16. *The New York Times,* November 2, 1916.

17. Harley Notter, *Origins of the Foreign Policy of Woodrow Wilson* (Johns Hopkins Press, 1937), p. 653.

18. A. S. Link, *Wilson the Diplomatist* (Johns Hopkins Press, 1957), pp. 15–16.

19. J. H. Taylor, *Woodrow Wilson in Church,* pp. 19-20.

20. A. S. Link, *Woodrow Wilson and the Progressive Era* (Harper & Brothers, 1954), pp. 81–106.

21. *War and Peace,* I, pp. 551–552.

22. See my "The Higher Realism of Woodrow Wilson," *Journal of Presbyterian History,* XLI (March, 1963), pp. 1–13, for further reflections on this subject.

CHAPTER 10. OUR CALVINIST HERITAGE IN CHURCH
AND STATE (HUNT)

1. Perry Miller and Thomas H. Johnson, *The Puritans* (American Book Company, 1938, p. 181.

2. *Ibid.*

3. Elwyn Allen Smith, *Church and State in Your Community* (The Westminster Press, 1963), p. 37.

4. *Ibid.,* pp. 37–39.

5. Arthur C. Cochrane, *The Church's Confession Under Hitler* (The Westminster Press, 1962). Also Wilhelm Niesel, *The Gospel and the Churches* (The Westminster Press, 1962).

6. Charles C. West, *Communism and the Theologians* (The Westminster Press, 1958).

7. This question was argued by the General Assembly of The United Presbyterian Church U. S. A. in its "Church-State Report." See the Journal of the General Assembly for 1963. The Smith book, cited above, is also an attempt to discuss this issue. Professor Smith was chairman of the General Assembly Committee on this subject.